Disneyland In-Depth

Discover the Magic! Mike Fox

Mike Fox

ISBN-10: 0998395072
ISBN-13: 978-0998395074

103121 - CS

To my wife, Kristy, and our two children, Brian and Megan. Let's all meet in our dreams by the popcorn cart in the Town Square.

DISNEYLAND IN-DEPTH

Includes In-Depth Details and Stories Not Found in Any Other Disney Books, Articles or Web Sites

- Learn about *The Disneyland News*, the now rare 24 page newspaper sold in Disneyland on Opening Day, July 17, 1955

- Discover what influenced a young 12 year-old Walt Disney to become an animator and how Disney Imagineers pay tribute to this within Disneyland

- Read about the now rare book Walt used to learn how to draw Oswald the Lucky Rabbit and Mickey Mouse

- Read about the careful restoration of Walt's beloved Lilly Belle miniature steam engine, one of the most treasured artifacts in Disney history

- Learn for the very first time about the medals adorning the neck of the "Cigar Store Indian" on Main Street, U.S.A.

- Read Disney Legend Bob Gurr's fun article about the debut of Disneyland's very first steam engine

- Learn how a Disneyland guest played a key role in developing two attractions, one at Disneyland and another at Walt Disney World

- Read for the first time ever the complete story behind the appearance of the very first Hidden Mickey

- With special stories from Disney Legends Marty Sklar and Bob Gurr, as well as Michael Broggie, Michael Campbell, Steve DeGaetano, and more

- And many, many more! All complete with photos, including many of rare Disneyland-related items!

TABLE OF CONTENTS

Follow Disney-Secrets Online

On the Web:

www.Disney-Secrets.com

On Twitter:

@149G22

On Facebook:

www.Facebook.com/DisneySecrets

(Look for the icon above)

INTRODUCTION

In my book, *The Hidden Secrets & Stories of Disneyland*, I reveal over 250 of the small "secrets" and story elements that the Disney Imagineers have purposely hidden throughout the park for guests to discover and enjoy. While most of those secrets are revealed with a story that is perhaps a paragraph or page in length, some are much longer, requiring pages for their interesting backstory to be told. This book, *Disneyland In-Depth*, combines the best of those longer stories with many new in-depth stories, quotes and photos, many of which have never before been published in any Disney related books, articles or web sites. Here, you'll discover for the first time insights about *The Disneyland News*, Disneyland's first newspaper, the never-before-revealed meaning behind the medals adorning the neck of the "Cigar Store Indian" on Main Street, U.S.A., (You never noticed he wore any, did you?) the first-ever-told story about the restoration effort behind Walt's beloved Lilly Belle steam engine, the never-before-published story of the man who hand carved "The Capitol of Disneyland"...20 years before the park opened, and many, many more, all complete with photos!

Enjoy discovering Disneyland...in-depth!

THE DISNEYLAND NEWS

The Disneyland News
OFFICIAL PUBLICATION — DISNEYLAND CALIFORNIA
VOL. 1—No. 1 JULY 1955 10c Per Copy

Disneyland's Main Street, U.S.A. represents turn-of-the-20th Century America. In this time, before the invention of radio or television, the primary means for obtaining news was the local newspaper, and every town across the country had one, be it The Times, The Tribune, The Gazette, or even the Picayune. Newspapers were big business and a very integral part of any town, large or small.

Walt knew Disneyland would be a very busy place with plenty of news to report. Tales of danger would come from such far away places as Adventureland, while reports of rocket ships launching for the moon from Tomorrowland would ignite the imagination, and accounts of harrowing escapes in Frontierland would captivate all who heard them. To convey all of this news, Walt wanted a monthly newspaper, something which captured the essence of the 1890s for Main Street, U.S.A., where it would be sold, yet all the news of today...and that newspaper was *The Disneyland News.*

In June of 1955, Walt hired Marty Sklar, a 21 year-old junior at UCLA and editor of the university's student newspaper, *The Daily Bruin*, and charged him with the task of coming up with an idea for the layout and execution of *The Disneyland News* and then presenting it to him.

"I went to work at Disneyland in mid-June, 1955 after my junior year at UCLA. Two weeks later, I had to present the concept for The Disneyland News to Walt Disney. Fortunately,

he liked it. Then we had to get it written, organized, designed and printed for Opening Day. Much of the written material for the first issue had been developed earlier by the Disneyland Publicity Department. I wrote some new, organized it, laid out all the pages, and interfaced with the printer. Fortunately, I knew a print shop to use in LA: they printed the UCLA student newspaper. We also found a print shop in Hollywood that had the old wood block type-faces we wanted to use for headlines. And I got support from Jack Jungmeyer, a Disney Studio publicity writer who wrote the wonderful 'Under the Gaslights' column." - Source: My interview with Marty Sklar

The Disneyland News
OFFICIAL PUBLICATION — DISNEYLAND CALIFORNIA
VOL. 1—No. 1 JULY 1955 10c Per Copy

Jim Schauer Blasts Off For Moon

Celebrities, Officials Join Walt Disney To Dedicate New Era in Entertainment

California Governor's Message.

Disneyland A 20 Year Dream.

Famed Cartoon Character Creator Long Envisioned Park Where Young And Old Could Find Happiness.

Congress Informed About Magic Kingdom.

Disneyland News Off Presses Today.

Year's Subscription Offer Available.

Soon, Vol. 1 - No. 1 of *The Disneyland News* was ready, and on Disneyland's opening day, July 17, 1955, it hit the newsstands for all of Disneyland's new guests to read and enjoy for only 10 cents a copy. From the front page of the Vol. 1 - No. 1 first edition...

Here it is, hot off the presses! It's the first edition of the Disneyland News, official publication of Walt Disney's magic kingdom.

All the answers to how Disneyland was created, the artists responsible for the drawing board work, and features on the four "lands" of the Park, along with articles on other Disney enterprises such as the forthcoming Mickey Mouse TV show, are contained in this and following issues of the publication.

In the early days of Disneyland, services for guests, including restaurants, refreshments, camera products, banking, stroller and wheelchair rentals, etc., were provided by "outside" companies, or lessees. The publishing of *The Disneyland News* was handled by Walt's newly formed Magic Kingdom, Inc., while its distribution was handled by two brothers, Joe and Ray Amendt, who ran Castle News at the park as a lessee. Their shop was located where The Mad Hatter shop is now, at the corner of the Opera House/Lincoln Theater building. Guests could buy *The Disneyland News* there, from newsstands on Main Street, U.S.A. or from newsboys outside the front entrance gates.

The front page of Vol. 1 - No. 1 featured a photo of Walt and Mickey Mouse aboard the E.P. Ripley under a headline, which read *"50,000 Attend Gala Park Opening."* Beneath, guests could read such stories as *Congress Informed About Magic Kingdom, Disneyland A 20 Year Dream*, and *Celebrities, Officials Join Walt Disney To Dedicate New Era In Entertainment.*

Inside its 24 pages were numerous articles about Disneyland's different attractions, how the park was built, the story book adventures of Fantasyland, a new Mickey Mouse newsreel, the upcoming

Disneyland Hotel, and much more, as well as ads for the different businesses found within the park, including Swift Market House, the Wonderland Music Store, Ruggles China and Gift House, the Red Wagon Inn, Yale Lock Shop, The Emporium and many others.

Of course, *The Disneyland News* was part of the story that is Disneyland, and as such, it not only informed guests, but also entertained them, and what could be more entertaining than to see your own name in the headline on the front page of *The Disneyland News*?! For 25 cents, guests could step into the Castle News shop in the Town Square and ask to have their name added to one of a handful of custom headlines, including "...Blasts Off For Moon", "...Visits Disneyland", "...Meets Davy Crockett!", and more!

Of all the stories within *The Disneyland News*, however, the best news of all was that guests across the country could now have their own annual subscription, as well as an informative Disneyland souvenir, delivered right to their front door for only $1.20!

Note: Marty Sklar re-enrolled at UCLA in September of 1955 to complete his senior year. He returned to work for Walt after he graduated and in time became the head of Walt Disney Imagineering, as well as the President and then Vice Chairman and Principal Creative Executive for The Walt Disney Company.

Rare Disneyland Newspaperboy Tour Patch
Author's collection

ANIMATED CARTOONS BY E.G. LUTZ

A 1920 first-edition, complete with an extremely rare dust jacket.
Author's Collection

Sometime in late 1914 or early 1915, a young 12 year-old Walt Disney sat in Kansas City's Wonderland Theater and watched a film, animated by Winsor McCay, called *Gertie the Dinosaur*. This innovative film was part of a vaudeville act performed by Mr. McCay, in which he stood on stage and interacted with Gertie as she lumbered onto the scene and began to consume trees and rocks, responded to questions, and drank an entire lake. This film had such an influence upon Walt deciding to become an animator that Mr. McCay is acknowledged today by The Walt Disney Company with a couple of tributes secretly hidden in plain sight by the Imagineers within Disneyland and Walt Disney World Resort.

While cartooning, in the form of comics and editorial newspaper cartoons, was wildly popular at the time, with Mr.

McCay's *Little Nemo in Slumberland* and *Dream of the Rarebit Fiend* being widely read in newspapers nationwide, the art of animation was still in its infancy. As a result, there was little which Walt could use as a reference or teaching tool at the time to learn the craft, as well as the skills necessary to pursue his dreams.

In 1920, Walt, along with Ub Iwerks, created a commercial art firm, called Iwerks-Disney, in which they produced ads for local businesses. This endeavor was short lived, however, and in 1921, Walt began creating animated films, which he called Newman's Laugh-O-Grams. During this period, Walt relied upon two early resources to learn and develop his animation skills; the *Motion Studies* volumes by Eadweard Muybridge, a pioneer in studying and photographing the motion of humans and animals, as well as a copy of a new book, first published in 1920, titled *Animated Cartoons - How They Are Made - Their Origin And Development*, by E.G. Lutz.

Animated Cartoons was the first book to provide readers with extensive knowledge about the art and science of animation. Its pages provided Walt with lessons on how to capture the nuances of anatomy and movement, as well as the effects of motion upon a subject. In addition, it explained in detail the science of animation and the equipment used to create a moving motion picture from thousands of still images. It is often said that "It all started with a mouse.", but before that mouse, Walt's early skills as an animator started with this book, which he relied upon to help create Oswald the Lucky Rabbit, followed by Mickey Mouse and other characters early in his career.

The Disney Imagineers' Tributes to Winsor McCay

Found in both Disneyland and Walt Disney World Resort are a few hidden tributes to Winsor McCay, the popular turn-of-the-20th-century artist, comic strip author, editorial cartoonist, inventor and animator, whose work was in high demand and known nationwide. Newspaper readers by the millions followed the surreal adventures of a young boy named Nemo in his Sunday comic strip, *Little Nemo in Slumberland*, as well as the surreal and sometimes all too familiar experiences in the strip, *Dream of the Rarebit Fiend.*

Disney Imagineers have paid tribute to Mr. McCay's significant influence upon Walt's life and career with the placement of a few story elements within the parks paying homage to Mr. McCay.

- Though not the patent holder, Mr. McCay was the inventor of the Mutoscope, a popular form of entertainment during the late 1800s and early 1900s. Users would peer into a viewer while turning a crank on the side of the Mutoscope, which would cause hundreds of still black and white images to "flip" by in rapid succession one after the other so as to give the impression of movement. It was one of the earliest forms of "motion pictures" and a precursor to the art and science of animation. You'll find Mutoscopes on Main Street, U.S.A. in

Disneyland, as well as the Main Street Railroad Station in The Magic Kingdom.

- Placed as a prop in Disneyland's Pixie Hollow is a large (4') jar of "Gertie's Liquid Glue", produced by McCay's Cement Company.

- Visitors to the shore of Echo Lake in Disney's Hollywood Studios in Orlando will find Dinosaur Gertie's Ice Cream of Extinction, housed in a building disguised as a towering dinosaur. More than just a nod to the Novelty Architecture of Los Angeles in the early 20th century, this blue dinosaur is an homage to Mr. McCay and his innovative animated film, *Gertie the Dinosaur.*

Drawing from the 1914 animated film "Gertie the Dinosaur"
Image courtesy of Billy Ireland Cartoon Library & Museum - Ohio State University

WALT DISNEY'S THE CAROLWOOD - PACIFIC RAILROAD

Walt with his Lilly Belle and the Carolwood - Pacific R. R.

Photo credit: Roger Broggie -
Photo used with permission from The Broggie Family Trust

The following is an article written by Roger Broggie, the first Disney Imagineer, for the very first issue of *The Miniature Locomotive* magazine, which was printed in May of 1952. It is reprinted here with the permission of Roger Broggie's son, Michael Broggie.

THE CAROLWOOD-PACIFIC RAILROAD, "The Fair Weather Route", is laid out on the side of a canyon on a quiet street in Beverly Hills, near the Pacific Ocean, in Southern California. It is owned and operated for pleasure, by Walt Disney, creator of Mickey Mouse, Donald Duck and other motion picture fairyland characters. Walt started his railroad career as a young "news butch" on the Missouri, Kansas and Texas R. R. and the

Missouri Pacific R. R., running out of Kansas City near where he was born. He has finally climbed the ladder of success, with an interlude of motion picture producing, to become President of this complete railroad, which although small in scale, is nevertheless "just like the big ones."

The train consists of a 1/8 scale miniature of a Central Pacific locomotive, six gondolas, two freight cars, two cattle cars and one caboose - all rolling stock is of the 1872-1880 period, running on 2600 feet of 7-1/4" gauge track laid out in a scenic pattern of trestles and tunnels along the edge of a canyon wall.

Walt's first experience with model railroading came with the construction of a Lionel train for a young nephew's Christmas present. He found this project a relaxation from his many duties as head of his studio. Therefore, he continued the hobby by assembling several locomotives and car kits in HO gauge and started an elaborate layout of an HO pike. But about this time, he had his first experience with live steam at Dick Jackson's one inch scale railroad in Beverly Hills. After an afternoon of running this train, the HO gauge pike was forgotten and a real LIVE STEAMER was born. He inspected and operated trains on several railroads before choosing 1-1/2" scale, 7-1/4" gauge as being the most suitable for his own layout. He liked the old time diamond stack locomotives of the 1880's for appearance and chose to follow a prototype typical of California. It was No. 173 of the Central Pacific R. R. built in Sacramento, California, in 1872, the first of ten similar locomotives built entirely on the Pacific Coast. Prior to this time, locomotives were manufactured in the East and either shipped to the West Coast by boat around the Horn or were shipped by rail after the transcontinental railroads were completed.

The Central Pacific No. 173

When Walt first contemplated building a steam model, he was surprised to find several among his employees that had experience with steam locomotives, both in full size and miniature. Among them are Ward Kimball, a top animator at the studio and owner of the Grizzly Flats R. R., a full size narrow gauge railroad, in his back yard in San Gabriel; Ollie Johnston, also an animator and owner of a 1" scale Pacific type steam locomotive and outdoor railroad, "The La Canada Valley Line"; Ed Sargeant, a mechanical draftsman at the studio with years of experience in miniature steam locomotive building.

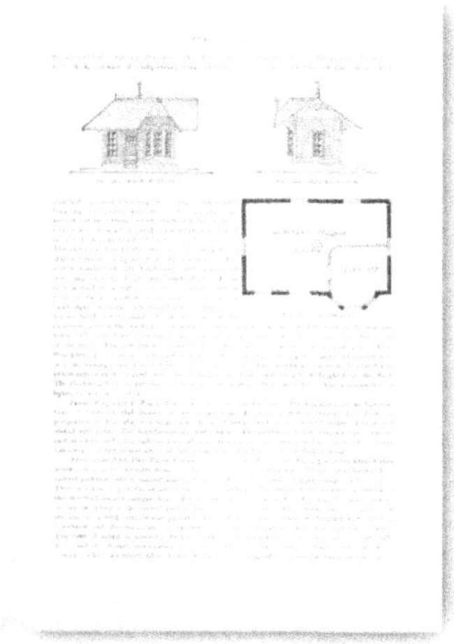

Books and photographs of early American railroads were furnished by Ward Kimball, Jerry Best of Warner Bros. Sound Dept. and a live steam enthusiast for many years, and Dick Jackson, Dean of all steam miniature railroaders of Southern California. Libraries and book dealers around the country were also combed for books. From this accumulation of data and a few blueprints from Southern Pacific R. R. files, working drawings for the Miniature No. 173 were started by Ed Sargeant in September, 1948. Patterns were also made in the studio prop shop by Ray Fox and George Bauer. Castings and fittings were made in the machine shop by Roger Broggie, Gene Foster, William Gillis and Dick Van Every.

Walt Disney came into the shop and learned to operate all the machine tools by making some of the parts himself. He made the whistle, flagstands and hand rails on the lathe. He learned sheet metal work by laying out and fabricating the headlamp and smoke stack. Then made numerous parts in the milling machine and learned to silver solder and braze on many small fittings. He now has a complete wood and metal workshop at his home.

The studio machine shop is regularly employed in maintenance work on cameras and other photographic equipment used to place the work of studio artists on theatre screens. Working on a part time basis, the shop built the locomotive and tender in time to steam up on December 24, 1949. A 300 foot test loop was laid on one of the Sound Stages and used for test runs until the outdoor track was laid. The locomotive was completed and cars made in 1950. The gondolas were made of cast aluminum by the shop.

Walt made the two box cars and cattle cars of wood in the studio prop shop, learning to operate all the woodworking machinery by doing so. He also made the caboose which is complete with running lights, bunks, clothes lockers, magazine rack with miniature newspapers, desk lamp, wash stand and a pot-bellied stove.

All the cars are mounted on arch bar trucks and are made up just as the original trucks were built. In fact, it got to be quite a saying around the shop that everything was "just like the big ones." We found that in following the practice of making everything just as it was made in the period of 1880-1900, gave the same kinds of trouble to us that the same equipment gave its owners in full size in the early days. Particularly this was true of arch bar trucks which are today barred on American railroads by the I.C.C. as being unsafe. We found them to be very rigid and liable to jump the track at any time. One reason for this was that as none of us in the shop had experience in railroad work before, we tended to make all fits too close, as we were used to machining parts for motion picture cameras and film equipment which generally have close tolerances. We did cure the tendency of track jumping in these trucks by making the side bearing plates free of the cars by about 1/8" on each side and making the center bearing loose in the center plate.

We approached the problem of laying the outdoor railway first as is done in full size practice but abandoned it for, what we termed the "Lionel Method" as being more practical. The layout was first plotted on paper at 1" - 20' scale. Full size masonite templates were made in 10' lengths in tangent and in radii from 45' to 60' in 5' steps and 100' radius, two templates of each required. The templates were laid on the ground, starting from the crossover point, and a record was made of the lengths of tangent and curved sections required to make the track go where the paper layout indicated. We tried to keep full 10' sections wherever possible since the dural rail comes in 10' lengths. The rail was rolled to the required radii in a set of motor driven rollers shaped to fit the rail contour. Then it was spiked to redwood ties in jigs. Ties were of scale section and length and rabbited for rail seating. They were also spaced in scale to full size practice. We dipped the rail spikes in a resin coating to make them hold tightly in the redwood ties and found it helped a lot. The rail was laid in all sections with a 3" offset and the track was bolted together in place on top of 2" crushed rock ballast. Ballast was added between the ties and tamped into place by a Mexican section gang who had had experience on the Southern Pacific R. R. laying track.

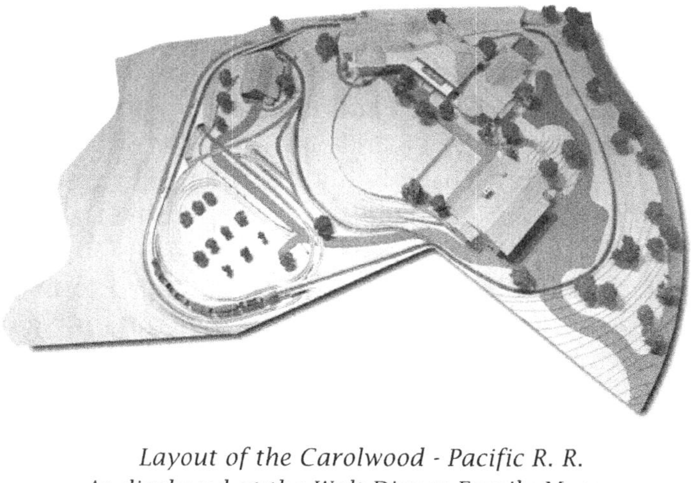

Layout of the Carolwood - Pacific R. R.
As displayed at the Walt Disney Family Museum

The first part of the railroad was laid in December, 1950, and consisted of a complete loop with a figure 8 inside, one passing track and one siding. It required eleven switches and one crossover to join all these sections of track and totaled

1200 feet. The balance of track, laid in May, 1951, is one long loop of 1400 feet which climbs from the lower loop with two connecting curved sections of track having 3 per cent grades. This upper loop crosses a 65' long trestle which is 9' above the track it passes over and runs through a 90' long tunnel. It also crosses three other short overpasses and a 20' long trestle that is 3' high.

All this combination of track, bridges and tunnel were necessary because of the contour of the land and to enable the train to run in either direction over any part of the track. This gives a total ride of over 5,000 feet without going over the same track in the same direction twice.

Switches were laid out to have tunnels at tangent sections of track and are right and left hand turnouts using a No. 6 frog. Guard rails and switch points were made from the dural rail, frogs were of cast aluminum. The switches were nailed up on ties that were first nailed down to diagonal stringers. The switch stands are a combination of hand and electrical operation. Automatic controls are also installed in the track. Contacts in the rail make it impossible to trail an open switch and a control in the tender enables the driver to select either to turnout or keep on the main line when approaching from the point side. All these controls on the track enable a person when alone to run over the complete system in any direction without getting off the train to throw switches and without danger of derailing at open switches.

A CTC board is mounted in a dispatcher's office which is part of the red barn workshop in the center of the railroad area. From this control board any of the eleven railroad switches can be thrown, enabling a dispatcher to send a train over any route he selects.

The complete electrical system, which was designed by Lee Adams of the studio electrical department, was based on the principle of safety and convenience of train operation. Most of the train operators are friends of Walt Disney. A lot of them are celebrities of motion picture, radio and television fields, who know very little of the intricacies of railroad operation; the CTC system and safety contacts were installed so that anyone could be shown the throttle and reverse lever and sent on their way around the track without fear of having them go through open switches.

A second locomotive is being constructed at this time. It is a 4-6-0 or ten wheeler based on the same period as the No. 173. In fact, the pattern and drawings of the No. 173 are being used on this second locomotive. The changes being in the frame length and rods. This locomotive will be used for freight hauling and a set of passenger cars and mail cars will be built later to go with No. 173. A third locomotive and train is planned for the future, possibly a more modern locomotive. So with three trains running on the track, a CTC system becomes necessary to control the running of the trains to avoid wrecks, which again is the reason for everything being "just like the big ones."

Restoring Walt's Lilly Belle

"Yes, in one way or another, I have always loved trains."
- Walt Disney

Walt Disney loved trains nearly his entire life. From his job as a News Butcher on the Missouri Pacific railroad as a 14 year-old boy in Kansas City to the trains he made sure encircle Disney theme parks around the world, Walt was captivated by these grand machines and everything about them. It is because of this passion that he designed and built, along with Roger E. Broggie, the very first Disney Imagineer, his own working 1/8 scale steam train, which he ran on a half-mile track in the backyard of his Holmby Hills, California home on Carolwood Drive. A line he called the Carolwood Pacific Railroad.

Pulling the rolling stock of the Carolwood Pacific was the Lilly Belle, a locomotive that Walt modeled after Central Pacific No. 173, an 1872 steam locomotive with a design that captured Walt's eye, as well as the historical essence of railroading.

As the demands upon Walt's time grew with the designing and construction of Disneyland, he found he had less and less time available to run the Carolwood Pacific. As a result, his beloved Lilly Belle steam engine was put into storage, moving to different locations before finally finding a home on display in Disneyland's Main Street Railroad Station, where it remained into the 1990s. On a couple of occasions through the years, the engine and rolling stock were crated and shipped for display at notable events, including at the Nixon Library, the Reagan Library and the California State Railroad Museum. Unfortunately, the rigors of time took its toll on the Lilly Belle, and it had incurred minor damage, with the paint becoming scuffed, parts being bent, pieces broken, and others missing entirely.

In 2002, Michael Campbell, then President of the Carolwood Pacific Historical Society, recognized that the Lilly Belle needed not only restoration, but also preservation, as it had become a highly revered and priceless artifact of Disney history. That year, Campbell created an exhibition that celebrated Walt's love of railroading at the California State Railroad Museum. This afforded him the opportunity to closely inspect the Lilly Belle and her consist, which served as the centerpiece of the show. He was concerned to see the deteriorating condition of the Lilly Belle: most notably, the hinged cab roof - hand-made by Walt - had split in two.

Years later, Diane Disney Miller and her son, Walter Elias Disney Miller, decided to create a museum that would explore and celebrate Walt Disney's remarkable life and achievements. They asked Michael to oversee all of the railroad-related exhibits in this state-of-the-art museum. Naturally, the Lilly Belle would have an honored place among the various displays. Michael realized that, with the museum scheduled to open in October of 2009, the timing would be perfect to have Walt's restored Lilly Belle included in the grand opening ceremonies of the museum. With this in mind, he proposed careful restoration of the Lilly Belle.

There were two distinct schools of thought regarding preservation versus restoration. The preservationists working for the Walt Disney Family Museum felt that the damage that occurred subsequent to Walt's passing were part of the story of the Lilly Belle and should be stabilized and preserved. The other approach, advocated by Michael, was that Walt poured great attention into the constructing of the Lilly Belle and that he was careful to have it beautifully presented whenever it appeared in photos or on film. Diane respected both viewpoints and was considering both until Michael shared with her an article that could help determine her father's intent. Walt wrote this article, entitled "I have always loved trains", for the October 1965 issue of "Railroad Magazine". The last paragraph of the article includes this statement by Walt: *'What happened to the Carolwood Pacific train? I still have it. I'm going to get it repainted and displayed in a glass case at the Disneyland and Santa Fe station.'* This proved to Diane that her father recognized the need to restore the Lilly Belle during his lifetime. Campbell later remarked:

"After all, out of all the things Walt Disney created, he only named one after his wife, Lillian Disney. It's hard to imagine that he would want it put on display for the world to see with obvious problems."

Diane asked Michael to work with the Museum staff to carefully restore the Lilly Belle. This included fixing a broken window and rods, bent fenders, repair of the cab roof and undoing damage caused by some large, ugly screws that had been used to secure the roof to the rest of the cab. The cab and other cosmetic restorations were performed by the Museum's Conservationist, Tonja Morris. Tonja's work was stunning; she masterfully erased all evidence of damage to the cab.

For the mechanical details, Michael contacted Sean Bautista, whom he knew shared not only Walt's love of trains, but also his attention to detail. Sean said he'd be more than honored to help in the restoration effort, so Michael introduced him to Diane Disney Miller, Ron Miller, and the Disney curators who would be overseeing the project.

Working from a set of original drawings, Sean cautiously and methodically undertook the restoration effort, carefully coaxing bends from the fenders, refurbishing the hoses to the Tender, realigning the pilot truck, and restoring the Smokebox. Throughout this, he would at times be struck by the significance of the project he had been entrusted with...

Walt Disney's Lilly Belle Locomotive

On display at the Walt Disney Family Museum in San Francisco

"There were a number of times in which I'd sit back in my chair, pinch myself, and realize that I was actually working on Walt's personal locomotive, the Lilly Belle, and holding in my hands the very same pieces that he himself had held so many years before."

Though a great deal of time had passed, in every piece he worked on Sean could clearly see the evidence of Walt's handiwork, as well as that of the Imagineers who helped him build the Lilly Belle.

"You'd be surprised how each Imagineer has their own unique and distinct style, be it Walt, Bob Gurr, Roger Broggie, or whomever. Just as different classical painters have their own unique brush strokes, each Imagineer who helped build Disneyland and the Disneyland Railroad has their own unique signature of craftsmanship, and I can study a Disney locomotive and easily discern the handiwork of those Imagineers who helped create and build it."

After months of careful work, Walt's engine was restored to the time of when he was at the throttle, and on October 1st, 2009, his daughter, Diane, dedicated the new Walt Disney

Family Museum in San Francisco with the Lilly Belle now preserved and on display for generations of Disney fans and guests to enjoy.

My thanks to Sean Bautista, Michael Campbell, and Michael and Sharon Broggie for their generous contributions to this article.

To read more about Walt Disney and his love of trains, I highly recommend the outstanding book *Walt Disney's Railroad Story*, by Michael Broggie.

THE RESTORATION OF THE LILLY BELLE

The following article was graciously contributed by Steve DeGaetano, author of the outstanding book "*Welcome Aboard the Disneyland Railroad! - The Complete History in Words and Pictures - Collector's Edition*"

In November of 1996, the *Lilly Belle* presidential car of the Disneyland Railroad was pulled off-line and put into rehab to restore and improve both the exterior and interior of the car, bringing it up to a "presidential' level. After this rehab, the car soldiered on several more years. But with every passing year, a new problem was festering under the surface: dry rot.

The car's wooden construction had survived decades of use, but now, the effects of moisture were beginning to take their toll. The exterior wood was becoming brittle and fragile, and in the late 1990s the car was once again removed from the line.

Unfortunately, those in charge of the Park were not too keen on spending a literal trainload of money to restore a car that few guests would ever experience. Even some pragmatic roundhouse cast members considered the car "dead weight" that added unnecessary tonnage to their trains, continuing to tax their already maxed out little locomotives. And so, once again, the stately observation car of the Disneyland Railroad was quietly stored away, out of sight, in the back of the roundhouse. There she remained, partially dismantled and windows boarded up, for several years, seemingly forgotten.

Various proposals by cast members to work on the car themselves came and went, and were sometimes the cause of inter-union disputes. Who should rebuild the car? The roundhouse crew, who primarily belonged to boiler or machinist unions, or Disney's union carpenters? All the while, the car continued to deteriorate, with one cast member commenting that the wood siding was so depleted in some areas that he could easily "put a finger" through it. Many guests may not have missed the car, but there were a significant number of knowledgeable fans who wondered about the beloved car that had so much history. Frequently, Disney-oriented Internet message boards had threads that asked, "What's the condition of the *Lilly Belle*?" or "Where's the *Lilly Belle*?" Clearly, folks missed her.

Everything changed in late April 2005. The Disneyland Resort had a new president in Matt Ouimet, who understood far more than his predecessors about the importance of "show" and "plussing" attractions. Ouimet was at the Park participating in a ceremony for Disney Legend and animator Ollie Johnston on May 12, 2005. At the conclusion of the ceremony, Ouimet was on his way back to the Team Disney Anaheim building, but made a detour to the roundhouse. He strolled up to the cast members in the roundhouse, and - according to one cast member there that day - made a simple, straightforward request: "I want to see the *Lilly Belle*."

Several additional inspections followed. Folks knew things were getting serious when Jeff Kaye, a representative of Retlaw, was asked to provide photographs of the car's interior so that an accurate reconstruction could take place.

Things happened rather fast after that. In the early summer, while the Disneyland roundhouse was preparing the debut of their newest locomotive, *Ward Kimball*, plans were underway to have the *Lilly Belle* sent off-site for a complete rebuild.

In August, a contract had been signed with Tim Lagaly of R. B. Builders, located in Camarillo, California, and the lovely presidential car was trucked to the facility to begin her five month rebuild. Lagaly won the contract for a very good reason: he had previous experience restoring the original "combine" of the train. Because of his hands-on experience, Lagaly knew all about the construction techniques used on the Disney cars.

The September 9, 2005 issue of the Disneyland Line contained an article on the progress, noting that the work "encompasses new siding and roof, refurbished mechanical equipment, and new exterior paint and signage. Inside, new carpet and refinished paneling and furniture will complete the restoration."

The car was returned to Disneyland the first week of December 2005, where work began to restore her interior. There were a few alterations to the car. The six rooftop vents seen in earlier photos were removed completely, as they had allowed water to enter and do damage to the roof. Brand new cast-brass nameplates, similar to the originals, were installed on the doors. A brand-new drumhead was created with the car's name. The black marker lamps, hand-made by Roger Broggie Jr., were found to be made of brass, so the paint was simply stripped and the brass polished up to make for beautiful "jewelry" on the car.

On the inside, the mirror on the left wall was removed. The original seats were reupholstered. New Disney family pictures were installed, as well as other knick-knacks, such as books Walt might have enjoyed and crystal sets. (all securely glued down to prevent theft!) On the back wall, authentic railroad lamps with the letters "GWR" (Great Western Railway) were installed. The brass-platted fans were made operable. Imagineer Kim Irvine, who once again oversaw the re-decoration of the car, wished to create a stronger connection with the car's namesake, Lillian Disney, so she found an old smoking jacket, very similar to the one Lillian used to wear, and hung it in the car. (This jacket is often mistakenly said to actually be Lillian's or even Walt's smoking jacket by some tour guides and conductors.)

On the floor, brand new carpet was installed. This led to more information that is often passed on by tour guides and conductors, who sometimes tell guests that the carpet is the last remaining piece of the original *Lilly Belle* carpet, and that it's the same carpet used in Walt's firehouse apartment. The carpet *is* the same as that used in the apartment, but the carpet there is brand new, too - that carpet was replaced years ago because of water damage, and the same roll provided for use in the *Lilly Belle.*

Another frequently repeated misconception is that the wood on the clerestory ceiling is inlaid with a different color wood, to create a unique design. The clerestory design is merely stenciled on with lighter colored paint. The fact that so many people mistake it for inlaid wood is testament to the skill of the Disneyland painters.

A month later, the car passed her roundhouse inspection and was attached to the rear of the Holiday Blue train an hour before Park closing on January 10, 2006, pulled by the *Ward Kimball*. Very few people were on hand to see her that late in the evening. The next day, she debuted in broad daylight, merely waiting to pass her DOSH inspections before she could begin accepting passengers. She initially made only dry runs, without passengers, while the conductors began their special training for the car. Soon, however, the elegant car would be open for passengers.

On the morning of February 15, 2006, prior to the Park opening, Matt Ouimet - whose concern about the *Lilly Belle's* condition nine months earlier had led to her renovation - would formally welcome the car back to Disneyland in grand style. The day was to be a two-fer - The *Ward Kimball* steam locomotive would also be dedicated. I (Steve DeGaetano) was invited to attend the ceremony by Tim O'Day, former head of Disneyland PR. I arrived early with Matt Walker, and we met O'Day near the roundhouse. We made our way to the platform at Frontierland Station, and I was introduced to Matt Ouimet. We shook hands, and Ouimet told me he had stayed up the night before reading my book on the Disneyland Railroad, so he would know what technical terms to use in his prepared remarks.

After Disneyland Ambassador Andrae Rivas introduced the event, the Ward Kimball whistled into the station, pulling a single Holiday Green car filled with Steam Train cast members.

Attached to the rear of that car was the *Lilly Belle.* Matt Ouimet spoke of Walt Disney's passion for trains and how that influence is still felt on the Disneyland Railroad. Following Ward's son John Kimball's dedication of the *Ward Kimball,* the honored guests were invited aboard to tour the *Lilly Belle.*

Sadly, Walt Disney never got to see the *Lilly Belle* built, but he no doubt would have been very proud of the work Disneyland accomplished in transforming the Grand Canyon into the sumptuous car.

Today, over 60 years after the *Lilly Belle* first took to the rails, we can once again enjoy seeing her at the tail end of one of the trains. The car that many believed would never again see the light of day now delights young and old alike with her Victorian splendor and detailing. While not all of us may get to ride her, we can appreciate the elegance of the car, and revel in the history she represents. Long may the *Lilly Belle* ride the rails of the Disneyland Railroad!

Walt Joins the Southern California Live Steamers

Many of Walt's inspirations for the Disneyland Railroad and Main Street, U.S.A. came directly and indirectly from his involvement with miniature "live steam" railroading. But while Walt had always had a love of trains since he was a child, his interest in miniature railroading would begin later in his life, during the late 1940s.

With the worldwide success of Mickey Mouse and his ground-breaking animated movies, *Snow White, Pinocchio,* and *Fantasia*, Walt was busier than ever as he managed his growing Disney Studios and a new slate of films during the early 1940s. Unbeknownst to him at the time, however, there was a new community of railfans dedicated to the world of miniature live steam railroading growing in the Southern California area, a world that Walt would ultimately find himself a part of whenever he stepped away from the daily rigors of his job.

On September 18, 1941, Dick Jackson and 34 charter members, including Disney animator Ward Kimball, Disney Studio draftsman Eddie Sargeant, and future Disney employee Dick Bagley*, met at the Sherman Oaks home of Mr. Bagley with the purpose of founding the new Southern California Live Steamers club, the first club of its kind in the state dedicated to the world of miniature "live steam" railroading. Soon, members began meeting regularly at 8:00 p.m. on the second Thursday of every month in the homes of various club members, and on one Sunday a month they and their families would gather in Mr. Jackson's backyard to run his 4-4-0 locomotive, the 900, and to ride his miniature steam train along his layout, the *Colorado Central*, which was one of the largest miniature railroads in the country.

1948 Chicago Railroad Fair - Official Guide Book
Author's Collection

In August of 1948, Walt, along with Ward Kimball, had the opportunity to attend the Chicago Railroad Fair, a mile long exposition on the shores of Lake Michigan which showcased 100 years of railroad progress. Immersed in all aspects of railroading for the extent of his visit, from historical locomotives to the newest "mammoth streamliners", Walt returned from the fair and told his wife, Lilly, "*That was the most fun I ever had in my life.*" Drawing inspiration from the fair, he was thrilled to see the possibility of combining his passion for railroading with his interest in miniatures, and as a result, he now set his sights on building his own miniature steam locomotive and railroad.

Shortly after they returned from the fair, Ward invited Walt to attend a "steam up" of his locomotive, the Emma Nevada, at his *Grizzly Flats Railroad*, which was located at his home in San Gabriel. Steam ups at Ward and Betty Kimball's place were festive affairs, and they were usually attended by club members, neighbors, friends, and even Hollywood stars and dignitaries, all in a party-like atmosphere as the coal burning Emma Nevada chuffed its way back and forth past a depot and water tank along 900' of narrow-gauge track. It was here that

Walt met Dick Jackson, the Founder of the Southern California Live Steamers, which had now been an active and growing club for seven years. With their shared interests in railroading and live steam, the two men hit it off. Walt no doubt discussed with Dick his new interest in building a miniature railroad, and in turn Dick invited Walt to visit his Beverly Hills home to see his *Colorado Central* and to operate his miniature locomotive, the 900. Taking Dick up on his invitation, Walt was captivated by all aspects of the *Colorado Central*, and it only furthered his enthusiasm to build his own backyard railroad. In the fall of 1948, with the help of Disney Imagineers Roger Broggie, Eddie Sargeant, Ward Kimball, Dick Bagley and others at the Disney Studios machine shop, Walt began the construction of an intricately designed miniature locomotive, one based upon the classic design of the 1872 4-4-0 Central Pacific No. 173.

While work on his locomotive and the corresponding tender and rolling stock progressed, Walt knew he would need some land on which to run his new train, so in June of 1949, he purchased 5 acres of property in the Holmby Hills area of Los Angeles. Here, he would have the room he wanted to build a new home, as well as new miniature railroad.

The precision machining and proper assembly of all the components for Walt's locomotive, tender, and rolling stock took some time, as the studio machine shop crew, which was normally creating and maintaining cameras and other photographic equipment for the production of Disney movies, was working on a part time basis on Walt's project, but on December 24, 1949 they steamed up the new locomotive for the very first time, taking it for a test run on 300' of track at one of the Disney sound stages. A little over five months later, on May 7, 1950, the beautiful *Lilly Belle,* named after Walt's wife, Lillian, made its official debut in the backyard of Walt and Lillian's new home and was soon pulling rolling stock and entertaining guests along 2,600' of 7-1/4" gauge track on a layout that Walt would call the *Carolwood Pacific*, named after the street on which he lived in the Holmby Hills neighborhood, Carolwood Drive.

The undercarriage of Walt's Lilly Belle engine, as it was being built at the Disney Studio machine shops. Of note is that Walt himself built the headlight and smokestack.

During the construction of the Lilly Belle steam engine and his *Carolwood Pacific*, Walt became a member of the Southern California Live Steamers club. It was in this club that he could step away from the pressures of creating such films as Cinderella, Treasure Island, and Alice in Wonderland, and instead relax and enjoy his passion for miniature railroading while socializing with fellow live steam enthusiasts, hearing about their different locomotives and layouts in development, and offering rides aboard his new *Carolwood Pacific.*

Walt joined the Southern California Live Steamers club in 1948, with his name first appearing in a 1950 membership booklet. The following image is a look at not only a set of very rare original booklets issued by the club, but also Walt's listing as it appears in the 1950 edition...

A collection of rare 1948 - 1952
Southern California Live Steamers membership booklets
Author's Collection

Walt's listing reflects the Disney Studios at 2400 Alameda Avenue in Burbank...

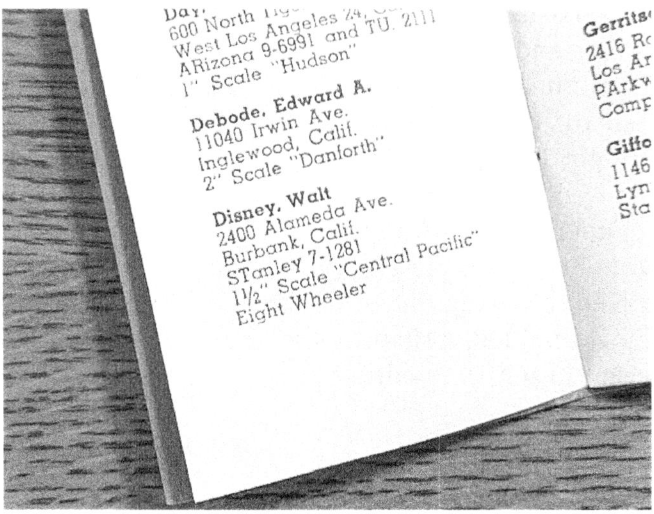

In 1953, an accident occurred on the *Carolwood Pacific* in which the Lilly Belle ran off the tracks and a young girl received some minor burns on her legs from a jet of steam emmiting from the locomotive. As a result of the accident, Walt put away the Lilly Belle and now turned his attention to an idea that had been percolating in his mind for quite some time, and that was of building a much larger railroad, one that would encircle a new theme park that he would call Disneyland.

* It's interesting to note that Dick Bagley was the founder of *The Miniature Locomotive Magazine*, in which Walt would place ads offering a "*Complete set of castings and drawings in 1-1/2" scale as used to build Walt Disney's own locomotive.*" The price of this catalog that Walt was selling at the height of his fame when his movies were making millions of dollars around the world?...35 cents.

WALT DISNEY'S OLD TIME RAILROAD

As part of Walt's passion for model steam engine railroading, he belonged to a community of like-minded enthusiasts, joining the Southern California Live Steamers group in 1948, along with Ollie Johnston. With the building of The Carolwood Pacific in Walt's backyard in 1950, members of the group, as well as other steam enthusiasts and the public in general, took note and were soon asking Walt to share details of his new railroad, as well as information so that they too may build a steam engine like Walt's new Lilly Belle. As part of the Lilly Belle's construction, Walt, Roger Broggie, and his team had acquired blueprints of the Central Pacific No. 173 from Southern Pacific and, through the work of Eddie Sargeant, converted these into 35 detailed drawings, which were used to build the Lilly Belle. Walt initially began providing these drawings to interested enthusiasts, but as demand continued to grow, he hired Dick Bagley to handle the growing number of requests they were receiving from fellow model steam train enthusiasts and the general public. Dick was a former President of the Southern California Steamers group, as well as the co-editor and publisher of *The Miniature Locomotive* magazine, along with Robert Day, and was charged with fulfilling the requests Walt was now receiving on a regular basis, as well as marketing the drawings and other items for sale. Soon, Walt had formed *Walt Disney's Old Time Railroad* and was placing ads in Dick's *The Miniature Locomotive* magazine for a $0.35 cent catalog offering a "Complete set of castings and drawings in 1½ inch scale as used to build Walt Disney's own locomotive." Now model steam train enthusiasts could order their own parts and build a model steam locomotive like Walt's.

DISNEYLAND
– A FABULOUS NEW WORLD

July, 1954 Edition - The Miniature Locomotive Magazine

Dick Bagley played an important role in not only helping to build Walt's Lilly Belle under the supervision of Roger Broggie, but also Disneyland's C.K. Holliday and E.P. Ripley steam locomotives, as well as the engines of the Mark Twain Riverboat. The following is from an article he wrote about Walt's new theme park for his fellow live steam enthusiasts in his *The Miniature Locomotive* magazine of July, 1954 ...

Disneyland...A Fabulous New World is Being Created By Our Friend and Brother Live Steamer...Walt Disney

The spirit of adventure has always moved people to explore new lands. In our present age the dream is of rocket ships and new planets, but the object of the quest is the same as ever: a land of peace, pleasure and happiness for all.

Such a place will be Disneyland - The $9,000,000 wonderland which is being created by Walt Disney in Orange County. The charms of this fabulous attraction, unlike anything anywhere else in the world, will be clearly understood and treasured in the hearts of children of all ages. The visitor to Disneyland will leave behind the cares and confusions of the world of today and enter a world of yesterday, tomorrow and fantasy.

I am honored to play even a small part in the creation of this massive project, and flattered that I have been asked by some of our readers to make first hand reports from time to time on interesting phases of the development of this unique center.

To start, let me attempt to tell you about Disneyland, although it is impossible to summarize in a few words. It has been defined as "a combination of world fair, playground, community center, museum of living facts and showplace of beauty and magic." It will be divided into four sections: Fantasyland, Frontierland, World of Tomorrow and True-Life Adventureland. Each will have exhibits, displays, rides, amusements and stores that carry out the theme of the particular area. In short, it will be filled with the magic and beauty that only the genius of Walt Disney could create.

Disneyland will be located on 160 acres of ground near the city of Anaheim, California. Approximately 60 acres will be used for the wonderland and the remainder of the space will be parking area for 10,000 automobiles. The opening is scheduled to take place in midsummer 1955. Meanwhile, heads and hands at the studio will be busy shaping the various wonders.

I have been lucky enough to see quite a few of them. There will be stage coaches, scaled-down replicas of those used in the Old West, accurate in every detail and large enough to carry passengers. There will be the giant squid, the sea monster that provides plenty of excitement in Walt Disney's newest movie, "20,000 Leagues Under the Sea." There will be a breath-taking monorail ride. Busy studio people, like Walt, will be able to commute from Burbank to Anaheim by helicopter. And there will be a train. Two trains.

That happens to be my department. Here, as everywhere else, Walt is the guiding light. The efforts of my crew and myself are to give him the railroad he visions.

There will be 6,010 feet of track on an eight-foot high embankment encircling the entire Disneyland. Visitors aboard the trains - one passenger, one freight - will be able to see all the features of the wonderland as they make the grand circular sightseeing tour.

One locomotive will be the same as Walt's 1½ inch scale "Lilly Belle," with which you are already familiar, and the other will be a modern version of the eight-wheeler. Passenger equipment will be the open vestibule type coaches used back in the 1890's and early 1900's. If that sounds too "modern" and comfortable, you can ride on the freight train, where you'll really rough it. You'll be herded through a cattle chute and probably share the space with a sheep or a goat in a cattle car - or you might be lucky enough to grab a perch in the caboose.

Scale for our railroad is 7½ inch to the foot. Track gauge is 36 inches, which gives us the distinction of being the first people ever to build a scaled-down railroad on a full scale. Or let me say it this way: We are following the design of standard gauge equipment and our trains will be much smaller than those commonly seen on a three foot track. Our trains will be cute, too - or else that helicopter may make a special trip to Siberia.

A Fair Inspiration for Disneyland

Disneyland is not the result of a single dramatic moment of revelation, but instead reflects countless instances of inspiration, ingenuity, and impressions which occurred all throughout Walt's life, from when he was a young boy in Marceline and Kansas City to later when he would travel around the world.

As a very young boy in the early 1900s, Walt lived on the family farm in Marceline, Missouri, and it is here that he developed an understanding of the personality of animals, the joy of drawing, and a sense of the small town that would ultimately inspire the look and feel of Disneyland's Main Street, U.S.A.

Later, in Kansas City, Missouri, Walt and his younger sister, Ruth, would make frequent visits to Electric Park, a meticulously landscaped and maintained amusement park which featured elements one will find in Disneyland today. As he strolled its grounds, Walt no doubt marveled at the elaborate carousel, penny arcades, shooting galleries, rental boats, flowering gardens, and chuffing steam train which encircled the park, all lit every evening by the magical glow of 100,000 electric lights adorning the buildings and many structures.

Travels to the great cities and places of Europe, including Paris, Nice, Copenhagen, and Zermatt with its Matterhorn, inspired even more ideas, as Walt strolled open boulevards, visited castles, studied the manicured landscaping and parterres, and even took notes about the features he admired at Tivoli Gardens, one of the finest amusement parks of its era.

But it was perhaps the 1948 Chicago Railroad Fair that provided not only additional ideas and inspiration for Walt's long-simmering idea of a theme park, but also the motivation to begin this project, which was now capturing more and more of his attention.

Chicago Daily Tribune

CHICAGO'S RAILROAD FAIR OPENS TODAY

BIG PAGEANT WILL DEPICT RAIL HISTORY

Old, New Trains in Major Roles

CARRIERS PUT ON 10 MILLION DOLLAR SHOW

Exhibits Cover 50 Acre Area

Visitor Has Wide Choice for Eating

Ideal Railroad Envisaged by Presidents of 3 Roads

Strip Diesel Engine to Bare Secrets

1948 Chicago Daily Tribune - Opening Day - Chicago Railroad Fair
Author's Collection

Located on a one-mile stretch of shoreline along Lake Michigan, and occupying over 50 acres, the 1948 Chicago Railroad Fair was an elaborate $10 million dollar exhibition celebrating 100 years of railroading history in Chicago and throughout the West. Running from mid-July through Labor Day, the fair attracted over 2 million visitors who took in countless exhibits, shows, and demonstrations sponsored by 38 different railroads, including "Wheels A'Rolling", "...one of the most spectacular outdoor stage productions ever presented in this country." Here, during numerous shows which occurred every day of the fair, 150 actors and actresses, along with 56 oxen and horses, 20 early automobiles, and a collection of colorful stage elements, would re-enact the important moments in the previous 100 years of railroading history, all with a great deal of pageantry.

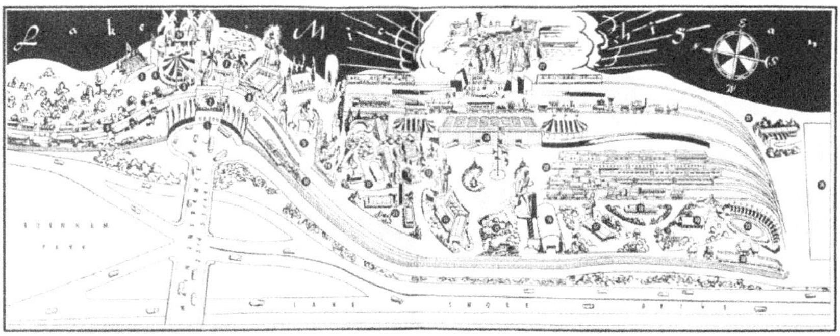

1948 Chicago Railroad Fair Map - From the Official Guide Book
Author's Collection

Back in Los Angeles, Walt was under more and more stress as he dealt with all of the demands of a successful growing studio. His personal nurse, Hazel George, suggested he get away for a while to alleviate some of his stress and to enjoy some much needed relaxation. He knew just the thing...the Chicago Railroad Fair. His wife, Lillian, and his daughters, Sharon and Diane, were sure to have no interest in such an event, so he approached Disney animator Ward Kimball, whom he knew shared his love of trains, and invited him to join him for a trip back east to Chicago to spend a few days immersed in the world of railroading history.

Taking the Super Chief from Pasadena to Chicago, the two were treated as V.I.P.s upon their arrival, and as such they were escorted from exhibit to exhibit as they took in every facet of the entire event. Along the way they ventured behind the scenes, ran prized locomotives, experienced the many exhibits, and asked questions of experts from around the country who shared with them every aspect about the world of railroading.

Inspirations for Disneyland began the moment Walt arrived at the fair. Near the main entrance, he saw the *Deadwood Central*, a narrow gauge railway traversing the one-mile length of the fair. Running an old-fashioned steam locomotive with a design like that of the Central Pacific No. 173, the *Deadwood Central* plied the tracks with old-time equipment reflecting railroading as it was in the late 1800s...*including a chattering telegraph instrument at the Central City station,* which is something guests will find today on the Disneyland Railroad.

Nearby was the exhibit presented by the Illinois Central Railroad in which visitors were transported to New Orleans, where they could experience a street scene and patio lifted out of the city's French Quarter. Walt no doubt walked down the quaint narrow streets and through the hidden courtyards, strolled through the tiny shops, noticed the balconies with their ornamental grillwork, and made note of the winding stairway, vine covered walls, and other reflections of the old south, all touches which ended up in Disneyland's New Orleans Square when Walt opened this new land in July of 1966.

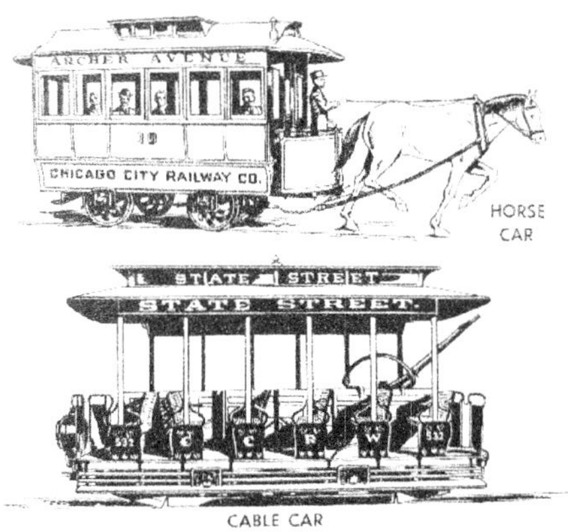

1948 Chicago Railroad Fair Image - From the Official Guide Book

Leaving the New Orleans French Quarter, Walt surely took note of the horse drawn trolleys, fire engines, and other nostalgic vehicles that not only contributed to the festive atmosphere of the fair, but also added a touch of old-fashioned America. Such nostalgic story elements would have resonated with his sense of patriotism and affection for the mid-west, both of which are portrayed today on Main Street, U.S.A.

Ad on the back of the 1948 Chicago Daily Tribune
Opening Day - Chicago Railroad Fair
Author's Collection

Near the 5,000 seat grandstand was the "Santa Fe Indian Village." Here, 125 tribesmen, women, and children representing six different tribes presented the culture of Native Americans on the western frontier. Housed in colorful adobe pueblos and other dwellings in a replica of an "Indian Village", including a trading post and curio shop, they performed legendary dances and sang age-old songs during performances given throughout each day of the fair.

In addition to the different exhibits, displays and attractions, Walt may have taken note of the layout of the fair itself. Arranged in a near linear format due to space limitations, it required visitors to walk back and forth throughout the fairgrounds during their visit so as to catch all of the many different presentations, demonstrations, and shows that occurred at variously scheduled times. This is a format that varies considerably from the efficient hub and spoke layout that Walt chose to use at his Disneyland park.

Greatly enthused by his visit to the fair, Walt wasted no time in moving ahead with his idea for a theme park, for on August 31, 1948, the very next day after he returned to Los Angeles, he wrote a memo to theme park designer and animation art director Dick Kelsey in which he outlined his vision for what would ultimately become Disneyland seven years later. Here are some excerpts from that memo, some of which reflect the same kind of story elements Walt experienced at the Chicago Railroad Fair...

The Main Village, which includes the Railroad Station, is built around a village green or informal park. In the park will be benches, a band stand, drinking fountain, trees and shrubs. It will be a place for people to sit and rest; mothers and grandmothers can watch over small children at play. I want it to be very relaxing, cool and inviting.

The Horse Car. The car would start at the Main Entrance and pick up those who did not want to walk. The car would take them down the street to the Railroad Station. The car would stop here for those who wanted to get off at the village or they could continue on to the Western village, then loop around and come back by way of the Carnival section; then on to the Main Village for a stop and continue until it was back at the Main Entrance.

We will have a Livery Stable where buck-boards are for hire. These will carry adults and children and will be pulled by a team of ponies which would drive them all around the village. Surreys and buck-boards will be available to go through the Western Village and the old farm. In other words, they can use any road. They will be rented by the half-hour, including the driver.

The Western Village. A general store with a soda fountain and lunch counter. We could sell most of the articles we have in the drug store in the village but we would also sell Western toys, Western outfits, toy guns, etc.

The Stage Coach. The coach would leave from the Western Village, pass through the farm, go through the Indian village and pass the old mill. This would be by a special road.

The Donkey Pack Train. The donkeys would be all hooked together and handled by one man. This would take ten kids.

DISNEYLAND PROGRESSES

Early Main Street, U.S.A. Elevation Drawing
As displayed at the Walt Disney Family Museum

Dick Bagley followed up his July, 1954 article with another in the September - October issue of *The Miniature Locomotive* magazine. In this piece, he gave an update on Disneyland's progress, with the park now less than one year away from its opening date.

Disneyland Progresses

By Dick Bagley

Dreams are now moving swiftly into reality. In many instances they have passed the blueprint stage. During the last month I have seen tiny gasoline automobiles whizzing around the studio lot being tested. Buggies of yesteryear, including stage coaches and surreys - with the fringe on top - are making an appearance.

In a movie studio you become accustomed to seeing strange sights. To find yourself in a setting of 100 years ago is not at all unusual. But to suddenly be confronted with a little red fire engine pulled by small horses as you walk down the street is another matter. For an instant you might think that besides going back 50 years things had also been shrunk.

There is activity everywhere. Walt Disney's workshops are busy. Somehow, I am reminded of the well known stories of the mythical Jolly Old Elf and his workshop in the far north where it is said that he is so busy all year preparing for the happiest of all days, Christmas. Not that I would compare Walt to Santa Claus, that is, except for his kind intentions. And in this respect, I wonder if anyone else has ever come so close to actually giving the people of this world the things for which Santa takes credit.

The Disneyland Railroad is fast taking shape. Two steam locomotives are under construction. Main frames were flame cut from one huge piece of steel. They are two and one-half inches thick and almost 18 feet long. Each weighs 640 pounds. If you have ever machined a set of frames for a small loco, then you would have enjoyed watching the apparent ease with which these frames were handled for finish work in the milling machine.

Many other parts for the locos have also been flame cut from sheet steel. For the benefit of those who may not be familiar with the process I will give a brief explanation. The flame is supplied by an oxy-acetylene cutting torch attached to a traveling crane. Thus the torch can be made to follow an intricate pattern and the whole works is propelled by electric power. Patterns to guide the torch may be made in several different ways. Ours were cut from paper and a photo electric-cell device followed around the edge of the cutout, thus directing the cutting torch. Steel cut in this way is smooth enough as to not require machining except for working surfaces.

Our pattern shop has already turned out a good truckload of the nicest patterns and core boxes that I have ever had the pleasure to see. Nearly all of the patterns required to build the locos have been completed. Most of the castings are also made.

Cylinders and saddles will be finish machined before this reaches print. They are cast in semi-steel. The design consists of three pieces, the two cylinders being separate from the saddle as was on the original full size loco No. 173. Cylinder Bore is ten inches.

Drive wheels are three-foot diameter and weigh 750 pounds each. They are fitted with standard locomotive hard steel tires. The wheel centers are cast in steel from our own pattern. Drive axles are chrome molly ground stock four inches in diameter. Side rods and main rods are also chrome molly. This material was chosen for these hard-working parts because of its great strength and ductile quality.

Engine trucks are made from bar stock in authentic copy of those used at the turn of the century but have been welded together, rather than bolted, to give added strength and safety.

The boilers are being built in a boiler shop according to A.S.M.E. code. They are welded construction. The owners of this shop and also their men have become so interested in our job that we are receiving all sorts of special attention. Everywhere I go the same is true. People in the various shops meet me with pleasure and each visit finds them more interested in locomotives than before. Most of them have never had anything to do with a railroad, but they are learning fast. There must be something contagious about this hobby of ours?

A great deal more has already been done. I would like to tell you about the cute little passenger cars that Walt is planning and lots of other things, but space is running out.

Full Plates for Disneyland's Birthday

"Happy 50th birthday, Disneyland Railroad"

By Michael Campbell

© Michael Campbell

The following article was written and provided by Michael Campbell, President Emeritus of the Carolwood Pacific Historical Society, which is dedicated to preserving the personal railroad legacy of Walt Disney.

The year 2005 marked not only the 50th anniversary of Disneyland, but the 50th "birthday" of two of its steam locomotives: the C. K. Holliday and the E. P. Ripley. These were built by Roger Broggie, Sr. and the machine shop crew at Walt Disney Studios in Burbank, with final assembly taking place at the Park in June, 1955. Although most of the Park was owned by Disneyland, Incorporated, the railroad was Walt Disney's personal property: he paid for the construction of the engines and their consists. The railroad cast members were employees of Walt's personal company, WED Enterprises (later, Retlaw Enterprises).

For unknown reasons, builder's plates were not created for engines 1 and 2 at the time they were built. Builder's plates are, in effect, the locomotive manufacturer's "signature"; they bear not only the builder's name but also the serial or construction number, date and location of manufacture, and sometimes the plant managers' names. They were found on virtually all steam locomotives and are highly prized by collectors. It always seemed odd to me that the Holliday and Ripley should be lacking this common yet vital detail. So, when Michael Broggie challenged the Carolwood Pacific Historical Society to think of unique ways to help celebrate the Railroad’s 50th anniversary, it occurred to me that we could "plus" the engines through the creation of custom builder's plates. Michael agreed, so I set about creating some designs to show Disneyland management.

Even though engines 1 and 2 are mechanically identical, great care was taken to ensure that each had a unique appearance. The C. K. Holliday was a reproduction of an 1870's wood-burning freight locomotive whereas the E. P. Ripley was a tribute to an elegant 1890's passenger train. It was important, therefore, to ensure that these plates would fit the individual style and era of each engine. Fortunately, I had the assistance of three of the most knowledgeable and qualified individuals to help determine the best design: Steve DeGaetano, author of "Welcome Aboard the Disneyland Railroad!"; David Fletcher, Master Modeler and railroad archivist from Australia; and, Jim Wilke, railroad historian and consultant to the California State Railroad Museum as well as to major model railroad manufacturers.

After many discussions and the review of dozens of photographs, we decided to fashion the Holliday plate after a Baldwin design of 1872. The Ripley plate, however, would follow the rectangular shape used by Rogers on an 1899 locomotive. Having selected the styles, we came to the much more difficult task of writing the verbiage. These two engines share the distinction of being the only steam locomotives built by WED Enterprises, the private company Walt established to manage the design and construction of Disneyland. (The other engines at the Disneyland and Walt Disney World are rebuilt Baldwins; the locomotives at the international parks were built by Severns-Lamb and other present-day manufacturers.) I decided to create the fictional "WED Locomotive Works" to take the place of the builder's name as a subtle reference to this fact.

We wanted to use the plates as a way to honor the history of these trains. On the Holliday plate, we included "Retlaw & Co." as the plant managers' names as a way to pay tribute to the fact that the railroad was owned and operated by Retlaw Enterprises from 1965 until 1982. For the Ripley plate, we listed "W. E. Disney, Pres." and "R. E. Broggie, Gen. Mgr." as an honor to the driving forces behind the creation of the locomotives. After careful consideration, we opted to assign the serial numbers "1" and "2" to the engines to signify that they were the first and second locomotives built by WED. (The fact that this matches the engine numbers is just a happy coincidence.) Having settled on the basic design, I designed some graphics that we could show for approval.

It's a rare occurrence that a group outside of the Company develops a "plus" for an attraction. As such, we needed to obtain permission from a number of entities, including Disneyland Park management and Walt Disney Imagineering. We were met with enthusiasm and support at each step through the approval process. Additionally, we solicited input and commentary from the group of people who best know and care for those engines: the crew of the Disneyland Railroad. Each group offered their suggestions on the style and content of the plate designs, and we are grateful for their support.

Although Walt Disney's family no longer owned the Disneyland Railroad — Retlaw Enterprises sold it and the Disneyland Monorail along with the rights to Walt Disney's name to the Walt Disney Company in 1982 — I still felt that it was appropriate to ask for his family's input on the project and for their permission to use the "Retlaw" name. I had successfully collaborated with Diane Disney Miller, Walt's daughter, and her family on various projects since the late 1990's, but I wasn't certain how they would react to this idea. Diane couldn't have been more enthusiastic about it! She liked the idea so much that she generously offered to pay for all of it. Disneyland had already allocated funds to this effort, so they didn't need additional support. However, I suggested an alternative way for Diane to show her support of the Railroad: we could create miniature pins of the builders plates and give these to current and past DLRR cast members.

© Michael Campbell

Diane happily agreed to provide these and wrote a note of appreciation that was printed on a card to which the pins were affixed. She suggested that we make more sets that were necessary for the Disneyland Railroad so that they could be given to cast members at other Disney Parks as well. I had the unique privilege of personally presenting these pin sets to the engine crews at Disneyland, Walt Disney World, Tokyo Disneyland and Disneyland Paris. The crews were both surprised and deeply touched that Walt's family continues to appreciate the dedication of the cast members who keep, in Diane's words, "these giants running and looking gorgeous."

To fabricate the actual plates, we enlisted the help of Harry Van der Wyk of Hortie Van Innovations. Harry has a long history with Disneyland: he and his brother, Lyon, supplied all of the flagpoles, banner and bunting to the Park when it opened in 1955. In fact, Harry would occasionally have breakfast with Walt himself! The foundry that Harry used has been in business for over 100 years, and they crafted superb plates.

The plates were affixed to the C. K. Holliday and E. P. Ripley in November, 2005. Thanks to the immediacy of the Internet, Society members were able to see photos of the finished product shortly after they mounted.

This project was truly a team effort. In addition to the aforementioned individuals, I must recognize: Matt Ouimet, Todd Bruechert, Eric Kratzer, Jon Storbeck and Ellie Marlow of Disneyland; Marty Sklar, Joel Fritsche and Barbara Hastings of WDI; and Diane Miller, Walter Miller and Charles Wixom of the Walt Disney Family Foundation. A very special thanks goes to Ray Spencer, the Imagineer assigned to this project, as well as Dale Tetley and the rest of the DLRR roundhouse crew. This tribute could not have happened without the collected talent and effort of these people.

Now you know the back story of how we helped create a lasting tribute to the 50th "birthday" of the Disneyland Railroad. So, the next time you visit Disneyland, keep an eye out for the builder's plates on the C. K. Holliday and E. P. Ripley. Out of the thousands of happy guests that day, you'll be one of a very select set who knows how they came to be.

THE FIRST IMAGINEER – DISNEY LEGEND ROGER E. BROGGIE

Listed on the builder's plate of the E.P. Ripley is the name of Roger Broggie, the very first Disney Imagineer. I would like to thank Mr. Broggie's son, Michael Broggie, for providing me with a biography of his father from his book titled Walt Disney's Railroad Story.

For almost a half-century, Disney's original Imagineer—Roger Broggie—worked in the entertainment industry. Among his many accomplishments were discovering the solutions for motion picture special effects, developing electronic robots that could sing and dance, and building transportation systems ranging from old-fashioned steam trains to futuristic monorails.

In 1939, Dick Jones was hired by Mickey Batchelder at Disney Studios. Jones insisted that he be allowed to hire Roger, who joined Walt Disney Productions as a precision machinist on October 1, 1939. The new Disney studio at Burbank was in its final phase of construction, and engineers were needed to move and adapt old animation cameras from the original location on Hyperion Avenue, in Los Angeles' Silverlake District, to the new facilities.

Roger's initial assignment was to install the complicated multi-plane animation equipment. Later he closely worked with Ub Iwerks, the Academy Award-winning designer of animation processes and camera equipment. Together, they developed rear-screen special effects, camera cranes, and high-speed optical printers: If Ub could imagine it, Roger would figure out a way to build it.

In 1950, Roger was promoted to department manager of the studio's machine shop, which had a staff of 12 machinists. Two years later, preliminary design work was commenced on Disneyland. A new company was formed called Walt Disney, Inc., to oversee the task. To avoid stockholder objections, the company's name was changed to WED Enterprises. Roger was one of WED's early leaders, selected by Walt Disney to guide Disneyland's development.

On October 18, 1990, Roger was honored by the Disney organization at a Disney Legend Awards ceremony along with six of his colleagues who "helped create the happiest place on Earth," in the words of company Chairman Michael Eisner. In recognizing Roger, Roy E. Disney—company co-chairman and nephew of Walt Disney—said, *"Any mechanical things you had to do, what you said was, 'Call Roger, he'll know how to fix it.' Without him, Disneyland wouldn't have happened."*

Photo of Walt Disney and Roger Broggie used with permission from The Broggie Family Trust

ORCHESTRATING THE STORY THAT IS DISNEYLAND

To Walt, so much of the story that is Disneyland could be found in the details. Circling his park are his magnificent steam trains, which purposely clank and clatter as they ply the tracks, just as with the steam trains Walt rode on as a boy. In Adventureland, the animals of the Jungle Cruise mustn't be still, but instead have to move and be active with every pass of a boatload of guests, and on Main Street, U.S.A., the music that fills the air is that of turn-of-the-century rag time played by the coin-operated player pianos, nickelodeons, and orchestrions of that era.

Disneyland is home to two orchestrions, both priceless mint-condition original working models...

The Nelson-Wiggen Orchestrion

Formerly located in the Disneyland Railroad Main Street Station, and now found in Frontierland's Silver Spurs Supplies, is the nearly 100 year-old 1927 Nelson-Wiggen 6 Orchestra Orchestrion. Featuring a piano, xylophone, snare drum, bass drum, banjo, cymbal and many other instruments, this original element of the Disneyland story provides guests with a taste of genuine musical entertainment from the days of when Mickey Mouse was being introduced to the world as Steamboat Willie. Drop in a quarter, and you'll hear a jaunty ragtime tune that differs from the more melodic orchestrial tune of the large Welte Style 4 orchestrion found in the Penny Arcade of Main Street, U.S.A.

But how did this rare musical instrument come to find its way to Disneyland? In 1953, when Walt was busy formulating his plans and designs for building his new theme park, he made a visit to Mrs. Ruby Raney, widow of Mr. Albert Clifford Raney, to look at his extensive collection of mechanical music machines, one of the largest in the country. With Mr. Raney's passing, she was looking to sell most of his machines, and Walt realized they may be perfect for his vision of Main Street, U.S.A. Upon seeing the collection, Walt was so impressed that he bought 30 different machines, including the rare Nelson-Wiggen orchestrion pictured here.

It's interesting to note that visitors to the Magic Kingdom in Orlando will also find a similar orchestrion, this one being built by the Seeburg Piano Company, also in 1927. In 1922, two employees of the Seeburg Piano Company struck out on their own to begin making their own orchestrions, unaware that their work would one day be seen by millions of people every year in a theme park in California. And their names?...Oscar Nelson and Peder Wiggen.

The Welte Style 4 Orchestrion

Standing in the back of Main Street, U.S.A.'s Penny Arcade is a stunning Welte Style 4 orchestrion that has been playing music at Disneyland since opening day in 1955. Manufactured in 1907 by M. Welte & Söhne in Freiburg, Germany, this elaborate antique provided the kind of musical entertainment enjoyed by Walt Disney as a child. Its collection of instruments features 265 pipes, as well as a bass drum, snare drum, timpani, triangle and cymbal, all while playing 75 key Welte roll music. Walt purchased this in 1953, and in 1955 it was installed in the Penny Arcade, where it's been entertaining guests ever since...just as Walt intended.

The following history of the Welte orchestrion is courtesy of the Mechanical Music Press. (www.MechanicalMusicPress.com)

From the beginning, Welte orchestrions were the premier automatic musical instrument of choice for royalty and the very wealthy, a trend that began circa 1849, when Michael Welte exhibited his immense automatic pipe organ, receiving generous critical acclaim and numerous awards for the device. At the time, his invention was an astounding advancement in technology, and reportedly the fame of the huge automatic musical instrument drew crowds from near and far. The public nicknamed the instrument "orchestrion", because it successfully imitated a many-voice orchestra. Since that time the term orchestrion has become synonymous with virtually any automatic musical instrument attempting to imitate a small to large orchestral ensemble. Thus it is that Michael Welte's early pioneering accomplishments in building spectacular, mammoth self-playing orchestras paved the way for his company's rapid climb to fame and fortune, with his handsome orchestrions being renowned on a worldwide basis.

Michael Welte began very modestly, after five years of apprenticeship with the master craftsman Joseph Blessing, by opening a small factory in Vöhrenbach, Germany, the town that was his birthplace in 1807. The little factory began business in 1832, with Michael Welte constructing musical clocks and other small musical cabinets on his own. The Welte firm prospered by word of mouth, quickly becoming well known and respected for not only the architectural beauty of its products, but for the quality of workmanship, too. In 1865, Michael Welte's oldest son, Emil Welte, established a Welte showroom in New York City, where he exhibited a number of large orchestrions, along with flute playing clocks, which the company still manufactured in small numbers. Immediately successful, or so it was stated by Welte advertising literature, the addition of the new American showroom, coupled with other already established markets for Welte products, soon compelled the company, in 1872, to move to nearby Freiburg.

By 1905 the line of products grew to include the soon to be acclaimed Welte Mignon Reproducing Piano, as well as retaining many of the older style products, such as the extensive line of Cottage and Concert Orchestrions. During the next few years, Brass Band Orchestrions, Philharmonic Orchestrions, "Brisgovia" Piano Orchestrions, residential pipe organs, theatre organs, home player pianos, and other related items would be added to the Welte roster. All in all, as most historians and enthusiasts of automatic musical instruments will concur, instruments built by Michael Welte & Söhne were among the most eye-appealing, magnificently ornate, and stunningly beautiful of all the large orchestrions manufactured. Thus, it is no wonder that they were so appreciated by the Royalty, wealthy industrialists, and fine commercial establishments that sought the privilege of owning a fine Welte instrument.

THE GAS STREET LAMPS OF MAIN STREET, U.S.A.

Main Street, U.S.A. represents a time of change at the turn of the 20th century. Horse drawn carriages are slowly making way for gas and steam-powered automobiles, store front windows are filled with the latest fashions, and single flame gas street lamps are being replaced with bright incandescent bulbs powered by the "new" electricity of the era.

A little known fact is that on February 7, 1817, Baltimore, Maryland made history with the installation of the very first gas street lamp ever used in the United States. Standing at the corner of North Holliday and East Baltimore streets, it dutifully performed its task for 180 years before being replaced with a replica in 1997. Being the first major city in America to use a gas street lamp, Baltimore had a large surplus of gas lamps available for sale by the time the 1950s came around, all with many different designs.

The often told story about the gas street lamps of Disneyland's Main Street, U.S.A. is that at the time Disneyland was being built, Baltimore, Maryland was selling its surplus gas street lamps, so Disney Imagineer Emile Kuri arranged to buy from Baltimore a number of gas street lamps, and it is those lamps you see in use at Disneyland today.

Walt hired Emile Kuri in 1952 as a set designer, and he would go on to receive an Academy Award and nominations for his work on Disney's 20,000 Leagues Under the Sea, The Absent-Minded Professor, Mary Poppins, and Bedknobs and Broomsticks.

With his eye for detail and style, and knowing the gas street lamps would be an important and highly visible story element of Disneyland, Emile no doubt chose the design you see today from Baltimore's stock knowing it would complement Walt's vision for Main Street, U.S.A.

It's interesting to note that when Disney Imagineers were designing the gas street lamps they would use on the Magic Kingdom's Main Street, U.S.A. in Walt Disney World many years later, they could have chosen a design from any one of the hundreds of gas street lamp designs which were in use across the country during the turn of the 20th century. However, they decided to chose a design with historical significance. The gas street lamps guests see lining the Magic Kingdom's Main Street, U.S.A. are *exact duplicates* of that first gas street lamp used in Baltimore in 1817, the very first gas street lamp ever used in America.

The Gibson Girl Ice Cream Parlor

Throughout Disneyland you'll find tributes to individuals who greatly influenced Walt Disney's life...the colorful antique Mutoscopes acknowledge animator Winsor McCay, a window on Main Street, U.S.A. recognizes Walt's father, Elias Disney, and with every frozen scoop of one of Walt's favorite treats, The Gibson Girl Ice Cream Parlor pays tribute to Charles Gibson.

Charles Dana Gibson was a skilled American illustrator best known for creating the "Gibson Girl", his personification of a woman who embodied feminine beauty and confidence during the late 19th and early 20th centuries, the period depicted on Main Street, U.S.A. His exceptional skills as an illustrator, especially those that conveyed the expressions of the human face in his prodigious work, were recognized and appreciated by millions around the world, including a young Walt Disney.

In addition, during WWI, Mr. Gibson led the Division of Pictorial Publicity for the Committee on Public Information, an agency of the government charged with influencing the public's opinion about the war. In this role, Mr. Gibson was involved with assisting military recruitment, and as such he lent his notable creation, the Gibson Girl, to those efforts, including in a poster which encouraged young men to serve in WWI as ambulance drivers in France. Coincidentally, this was the position Walt held after joining the Red Cross Ambulance Corp at the age of 16, in which he spent one year in France, from 1918 to 1919, driving supplies from warehouses to hospitals and canteens in and around Paris, as well as the surrounding French countryside.

Of note is that only two Disney theme parks in the world include a Gibson Girl Ice Cream Parlor; Disneyland and, of course, Disneyland Paris.

Walt as a Red Cross Ambulance Corp driver in France
Photo courtesy of The Walt Disney Family Museum

CRYSTAL ARTS
&
THE ARRIBAS BROTHERS

Step into the Crystal Arts shop on Main Street, U.S.A., opposite the Gibson Girl Ice Cream Parlor, and you enter into a world of history reaching directly back to Walt and the early days of Disneyland, as well as nearly 100 years ago to the small town of La Coruña, Spain, for it was here that Tomas Arribas was born in 1930, followed by his younger brother, Alfonso, in 1936. As young men they studied the old-world skills of glassblowing, a craft practiced by their family for generations, which was now being passed down to them both. In time, they developed such skill and mastery of the art that they began to acquire a reputation for their fine work, and in 1963 the two of them were approached by the Spanish Cultural Ministry to represent Spain in a pavilion at the 1964 / 1965 Worlds Fair, to be held in New York.

Comprised of three interconnected buildings, the Spanish Pavilion was hailed as the "Jewel of the New York World's Fair", showcasing Spain's rich cultural heritage. Historical artifacts, oil painting masterpieces, priceless sculptures by world-renowned artists, stunning treasures, innovative technology, and of course glassblowing exhibits drew millions of visitors to one of the most popular pavilions at the fair. Among these visitors was Walt Disney himself, and he was so taken by the impressive glassblowing skills and resulting artwork of Tomas and Alfonso, that it was decided that the Arribas brothers would open a glassblowing shop at Disneyland.

The 1964 / 1965 New York World's Fair ran through October of 1965, and in June of 1967, the Arribas brothers opened their first glassblowing studio in a small shop inside Sleeping Beauty Castle. Though tucked out of the way, guests were just as impressed with the glasswork as Walt was, and in time the shop was moved to Main Street, U.S.A., where it has been a classic Disneyland attraction ever since. Today, guests can purchase Disney characters, crystal art pieces, small jewelry, impressive large sculptures, shimmery tiaras, and many other hand-crafted souvenirs at 19 different Arribas Brothers shops found at Disney parks and properties around the world.

WALT'S EDISON SQUARE

1962 Souvenir Map of Disneyland

As guests stand on Disneyland's Plaza Street, they may be wondering, "Where does it go?" The answer?...To an important piece of Disneyland history that never was.

Walt Disney had imagined at the end of Plaza Street a walk-through attraction he called Edison Square, which was to be a tribute to Thomas A. Edison, the prolific American inventor who not only changed the face of the world and the course of history, but also invented many of the technologies which helped Walt bring his stories to life, including the motion picture camera, recorded music and the phonograph.

In a WED proposal to General Electric, Walt Disney explained his vision for Edison Square...

"*Edison Square in Disneyland will dramatically present the story of the way in which one invention by Thomas A. Edison has influenced the growth and development of America...Edison Square is the story of that era: the birth, growth, development and future of electricity and General Electric products.*

Located just a few steps from Main Street, Edison Square will be the passing of the 'old' of the 19th century to the 'new' of the 1900s. As they enter Progress Place in Edison Square, where they will find that 'Progress Is Our Most Important Product', visitors will see two separate plaques on which General Electric's symbol and appropriate words setting forth the theme of Edison Square will appear.

Inside the buildings, General Electric's theatrical productions will be staged for Disneyland visitors. Edison Square will be alive and vital. Disneyland's horseless carriages' and surreys which travel up and down Main Street will move in and out of the area. Such annual Disneyland special events as the 'Horseless Carriage Day Parade' and the 'Easter Parade' will be part of Edison Square.

The square itself will be architecturally landscaped befitting the turn-of-the-century. It will contain the 'new' electric lamps, iron grill work, hitching posts and other 'signs of the times.' All the windows in the buildings will be authentically dressed and specially lighted to carry out the atmosphere of the area."

Among the many wonders Walt wanted to showcase in Edison Square was a life-sized statue of Thomas Edison, something no doubt similar to the "Partners" statue of Walt and Mickey Mouse found today in front of Sleeping Beauty Castle.

INTERNATIONAL STREET

Photo courtesy of www.davelandweb.com

"Disneyland will never be completed. It will continue to grow as long as there is imagination left in the world."
- Walt Disney

Walt knew his new Disneyland had to continually grow and change so as to always provide magical new experiences for his guests with each and every visit. Seventeen different attractions welcomed guests on opening day in 1955, but of course many more would follow as Disneyland's story continued to unfold, including Dumbo the Flying Elephant, the Matterhorn Bobsleds, "it's a small world", Pirates of the Caribbean, the Haunted Mansion and others. Unfortunately, two of Walt's ideas never came to fruition; International Street and Liberty Street.

Before you head down Main Street, U.S.A. toward Sleeping Beauty Castle, make your way towards the Mad Hatter and take note of the short "road spur" in front of the shop. Today, this road leads to a backstage area, but in 1955 Walt had plans for it to lead to an all new "land" in the park, one called International Street.

Like Main Street, U.S.A., but with an international flavor instead of old-fashioned American, International Street would allow guests to walk its narrow winding street amidst shops, restaurants and exhibits from around the world, as well as enjoy entertainment with an international flair. Many feel International Street was a precursor of Epcot's World Showcase, as guests would've moved "from country to country" as they made their way along. However, just as International Street began to materialize in its planning and construction phase, Walt would begin production on a new Disney movie about the revolutionary times in Colonial America, titled "Johnny Tremain", which caused him to think of a different use for this space...a new land he would call "Liberty Street."

WALT'S LIBERTY STREET

Photo courtesy of www.davelandweb.com

Walt was very appreciative and respectful of our country's heritage, and he sought to reflect this in his new Disneyland. On opening day in July, 1955, he had included both Town Square and Main Street, U.S.A., two attractions which reflect a time in America's history of simple, honest values, as well as Frontierland, with its nod to the courage of discovery in the old West.

In September of 1956, a little over one year after Disneyland had opened, Walt began production on a new movie titled "Johnny Tremain", which told the story of a young man by the same name who worked as a silversmith apprentice in Boston alongside Paul Revere. Set in Colonial America in the year 1775, Johnny plays an important role in a number of famous events which culminated in the American Revolution, including the Boston Tea Party and Paul Revere's ride warning "The British are coming!"

In reading the story as preparation for the film, Walt realized he had made an oversight in planning his new theme park...

"After reading Johnny Tremain, we realized we had overlooked one major item in the blueprint of Disneyland. A memorial to the freedoms that made it all possible."

With this, Walt began to rethink his plans for what was then International Street off of Town Square. He realized he now wanted this street to be a representation of Colonial America, an area of the park in which guests could acquire an understanding and appreciation of the Revolutionary War, our nation's Presidents, how enterprise helped shape our great country and the dramatic struggles and events which won us all liberty and freedom. Walt said...

"Liberty Street will be Johnny Tremain's Boston of about 1775."

Designed as a cul-de-sac instead of a long winding street, Liberty Street would welcome guests with a collection of attractions, shops and exhibits which immersed them in colonial times. A glass shoppe would feature working glass smiths hand blowing colorful pieces of art, while nearby a blacksmith would be practicing his trade, and of course, Paul Revere's Silver Shop would welcome guests with the finest examples in the art of Silversmithing.

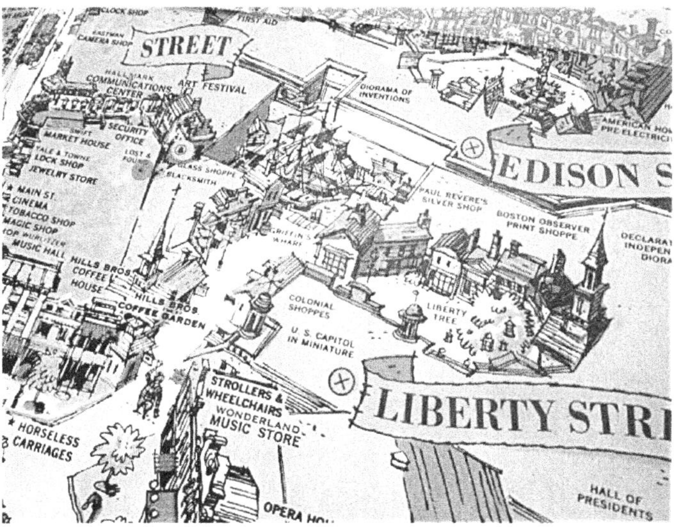

1962 Sam McKim Souvenir Map of Disneyland

Two authentic three-masted ships at Griffin's Wharf would "anchor" one end of Liberty Street, while stately Liberty Hall would majestically reside at the other. Inside, a show titled, "One Nation Under God", would feature Walt's earliest attempts at Audio-Animatronic figures of our nation's Presidents, a technology which he would soon perfect and reveal to the world at The Enchanted Tiki Room in 1963 and the 1964 New York World's Fair.

While Liberty Street was never built, many of Walt's concepts and dreams for this land were developed for use elsewhere in Disneyland, as well as all throughout Liberty Square in Walt Disney World's Magic Kingdom.

Bonus Story - Dispelling a Myth about the Liberty Bell

Found near the Liberty Tree in *Walt Disney World's Magic Kingdom* is a life-sized replica of the historic Liberty Bell, the original of which hangs today in the Liberty Bell Center in Independence National Historical Park in Philadelphia, Pennsylvania.

Around the top of the bell are the words...

PROCLAIM LIBERTY THROUGHOUT ALL THE LAND UNTO ALL THE INHABITANTS THEREOF LEV. XXV. V X – BY ORDER OF THE ASSEMBLY OF THE PROVINCE OF PENSYLVANIA FOR THE STATE HOUSE IN PHILAD.A

Astute guests will notice that the word "Pensylvania" appears to be misspelled on the bell. However, this isn't a mistake, but instead it's another example of Disney's level of attention to historical detail found throughout Liberty Square and Disney theme parks around the world.

So how did this spelling come about originally?

In 1751, the Pennsylvania Assembly sought to obtain a large bell that could be heard all throughout the small but growing town of Philadelphia, as the current bell, purportedly brought to America by William Penn and hung in a tree outside the meeting place of the Pennsylvania colonial assembly, was proving to be too small to be heard to the town's limits when rung. In turn, the Assembly commissioned London's Whitechapel Bell Foundry to cast the new bell, which was to be known as the Pennsylvania State House Bell. Messrs. Isaac Norris, Thomas Leech and Edward Warner all signed the commission for the bell and directed that it should be "...shipped with the following words well shaped in large letters round it viz"...

BY order of the Assembly of the Province of Pensylvania for the State house in the City of Philad.a 1752 - Proclaim Liberty thro' all the Land to all the inhabitants thereof Levit. XXV. 10.

So at the hand of Messers. Norris, Leech and Warner the spelling of Pensylvania with only two "n"s originated, as this was considered to be acceptable at that time.

Shortly after the bell's arrival in Philadelphia, it was discovered that the bell had suffered a crack, either in transit to America or upon its first ringing. Instead of having the bell shipped back to the Whitechapel Foundry, the Pennsylvania Assembly commissioned two Philadelphia men, John Pass and John Stow, to create an entirely new bell using the metal of the original one. Lacking the proper facilities of the Whitechapel Foundry, the two men broke the original bell into smaller pieces, melted them down and then recast the new bell with a similar design, though with a slightly different inscription, which read:

PROCLAIM LIBERTY THROUGHOUT ALL THE LAND UNTO ALL THE INHABITANTS THEREOF LEV. XXV. V X – BY ORDER OF THE ASSEMBLY OF THE PROVINCE OF PENSYLVANIA FOR THE STATE HOUSE IN PHILAD.A

PASS AND STOW

PHILAD.A

MDCCLIII

Upon the new bell's completion, it was hung in the tower of the State House, later known as Independence Hall. However, the citizens did not like the tone of the new bell, so they requested Pass and Stow recast the bell once again. The second casting was a success, and it was this second bell that would go on to become known worldwide as the Liberty Bell.

22 Shiny New Liberty Bell Replicas - 1950 - Paccard Fonderie, France

It is interesting to note that many Liberty Bell replicas, including that in the Magic Kingdom, make the claim that they were cast from the same mold as the original Liberty Bell of either 1751 or 1752. However, this is highly unlikely, as bells manufactured in the mid-1700s were cast using fragile molds made of clay, horse hair, loam and horse manure, and in the case of the Pass and Stow bell, the mold using these elements was formed within a hole dug into the ground. Because the original 1751 bell and the ensuing Pass and Stow bell of 1752 had not achieved historical significance at the time of their casting, it is highly unlikely that much thought would have been given at the time to keeping either of these original fragile molds, let alone arranging to have them preserved for well over 200 years so they may be used in the 20th century. If this were to have occurred, then these same molds would still be preserved today, yet the molds, or even photos of them, do not exist.

Part of the confusion arises from a number of replicas made of the 1752 Pass and Stow bell. In 1950, President Harry Truman created a savings bond campaign to pay for the casting of approximately 56 Liberty Bell replicas by the Paccard Fonderie in Annecy Le Vieux, France. These replicas were from all new molds, using the Pass and Stow Liberty Bell as a *guide*, and because they were created by the large and well-equipped Paccard Foundry in 1950 instead of two men in a small foundry in 1752, the bells exhibited a more polished and refined exterior, differing greatly from the somewhat crude and rough exterior of the original Pass and Stow Liberty Bell. Guests will notice that the Magic Kingdom's Liberty Square Liberty Bell, which was cast in 1989, reflects the more refined exterior of its contemporary casting.

Source: Interview with Robert Giannini III - Museum Curator - Independence National Historical Park - Philadelphia, PA

"The Liberty Bell of Independence National Historical Park: A Special History Study - John C. Paige.

Liberty Bell photo courtesy of WDWGuidedTours.com

1950 Postcard photo of 22 Liberty Bells - Author's collection

DISNEYLAND'S CIGAR STORE INDIANS

As you make your way up Main Street, U.S.A. in either Disneyland or The Magic Kingdom, you'll see to the right what is known as the "Cigar Store Indian." During the turn of the previous century, before the Internet, television and even radio, shop owners had to rely upon their store front as their primary means of advertising. For some stores, their efforts went beyond their store front windows and carried out onto the sidewalk. A striped barber pole conveyed the services of a barber, while a clock advertised the wares of a jewelry store, and a pestle and mortar indicated the services of a Pharmacist. In the case of Main Street, U.S.A.'s Cigar Store Indians, these advertise former Tobacco shops, which sold cigars, cigarettes, matches and other tobacco related items to guests in the early days of each park, with the Fine Tobacco shop selling to guests in Disneyland and the Tobacconist Shop selling to guests in the Magic Kingdom.

According to the Disney Archives, these Cigar Store Indians, as well as those you will find in Frontierland of each park, do not have names. While we do not know much at all about these "characters" within the story of the parks, we do know that they are important Native Americans, not only within there own tribes, as evidenced by their feathered headdresses, but also when it comes to negotiations for peace with the U.S. Government. What is the evidence of this? The large Peace Medals found hanging around their necks.

Often overlooked by guests, the Native American statue in *The Magic Kingdom* is wearing two Peace Medals. The one in front displays the image of James A. Garfield and reads, "President of the United States 1881", while the other depicts an image of a farmer and his family greeting a Native American at their homestead, all below the word "Peace." These two medals are actually the obverse and reverse of the single James Garfield Indian Peace Medal. Commissioned by different U.S. Presidents and reflecting various designs, Peace Medals such as these were offered by representatives of the U.S. Government to Chiefs and other Native American leaders during the 1700s and 1800s as a symbol of respect during the signing of peace treaties and other important ceremonies. In turn, the recipients would often hang them around their necks as a symbol of their stature.

The Peace Medal adorning the Cigar Store Indian statue in Disneyland features the likeness of George Washington, though it is lacking descriptive detail. In addition, it does not appear to be fashioned after a specific medal, as is the case with the President Garfield Peace Medal in The Magic Kingdom.

STEAMBOAT WILLIE - MICKEY MOUSE'S 3RD CARTOON

If you were to ask someone the name of Mickey Mouse's first cartoon, chances are they will tell you it was *Steamboat Willie.* While this is a good answer, it's actually incorrect. On May 15, 1928, Walt Disney gave a test screening in Hollywood of Mickey Mouse's very first cartoon, *Plane Crazy*, a silent film inspired by the daring adventures of Charles Lindberg, who, in 1927, became the first man to make a non-stop solo flight across the Atlantic ocean. Unfortunately, as a silent film, and perhaps because nobody had ever heard of Mickey Mouse at that point, the film failed to pick up a distributor. His second film, The Gallopin' Gaucho, was released on August 7th, 1928, and with it being a silent film, as well, it also had trouble finding a distributor.

Walt, realizing the importance of sound, introduced Mickey Mouse to the world three months later, on November 18, 1928, in the first synchronized post-produced sound cartoon, *Steamboat Willie.*

"Sound effects and talking pictures are more than a mere novelty. They are here to stay. The ones that get in on the ground floor are the ones that will more likely profit by its future development."

- Walt Disney, September 14, 1928

These three cartoons not only introduced Mickey Mouse to the world, but also launched Disney Cartoons and what would become The Walt Disney Company, the largest media and entertainment company in the world.

Note: According to the Disney Archives, Mickey Mouse's birth date "*...has always been determined to be the date that Steamboat Willie opened at the Colony Theater.*", which was November 18, 1928.

DISNEYLAND'S AUTOPIA

Of all the attractions in Disneyland's Tomorrowland, perhaps none generates the real-world excitement for those too young to drive as Autopia. Here, young guests get the opportunity to hop into the front seat of a real car and drive with the top down on a Disneyland freeway.

Anything which moves guests at Disneyland, including the Monorail, the Matterhorn Bobsleds, and the Doombuggies of the Haunted Mansion, was designed by Disney Legend Bob Gurr, and shortly after being hired in 1954, Bob was charged with designing and building Disneyland's new Autopia cars. Utilizing his design and engineering skills developed while working at the Ford Motor Company, Bob first designed the cars on paper, and then, with the assistance of students at the Art Center College of Design in Pasadena, California, progressed to creating a full-sized model of a car out of clay, which is called a "clay buck." From the clay buck, a mold is then made, which in turn is used to create the final vehicle.

The clay buck was built in the North Hollywood garage of Joe Thompson, one of the teachers at the Art Center College of Design, and after it was finished, Bob needed Walt to approve the design. However, being new to the company, he

figured a big, important studio head would never come over to someone's garage, so he asked Walt if he could bring the clay model over to the studio for approval, to which Walt replied, "*You're going to bring that big heavy thing over here just so I can look at it? Nonsense. We can all drive there in a few minutes.*" So Roger Broggie, Dick Irvine, Bill Cottrell, Bob and Walt all piled into a car and headed over to the garage. Once there, Walt sat down in the clay buck. Unfortunately, the clay was still sticky, so Walt ended up with it all over his jacket, but he liked Bob's design and approved the car for production.

In the words of Bob Gurr..."*I never saw Walt act like a big-shot. He had high standards of excellence, but he was never demanding. He never wanted people to go out of their way just to serve him. Fact is, he would go out of his way to save time for us, and that made everything go more smoothly.*"

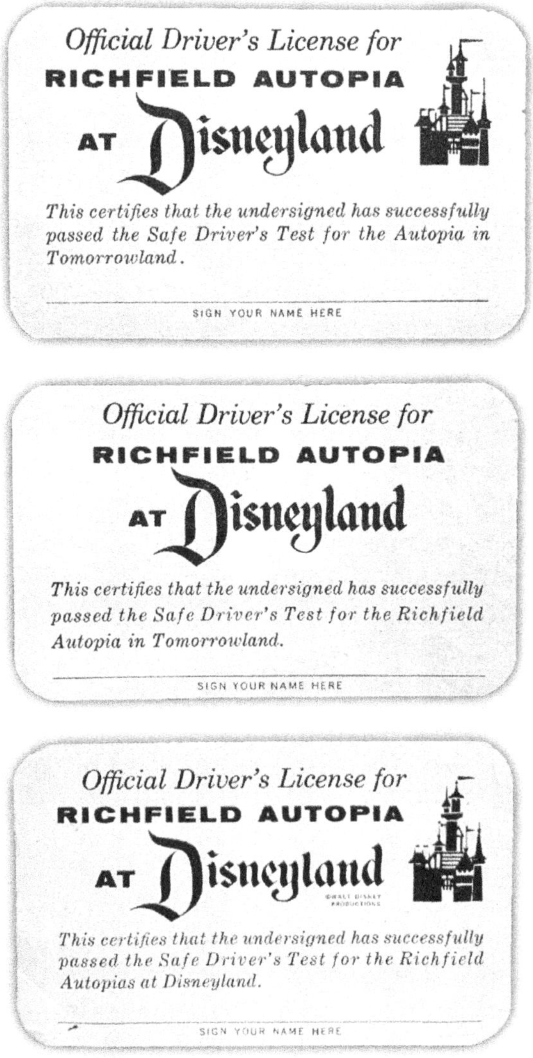
Official Driver's License for
RICHFIELD AUTOPIA
AT Disneyland

This certifies that the undersigned has successfully passed the Safe Driver's Test for the Autopia in Tomorrowland.

SIGN YOUR NAME HERE

Official Driver's License for
RICHFIELD AUTOPIA
AT Disneyland

This certifies that the undersigned has successfully passed the Safe Driver's Test for the Richfield Autopia in Tomorrowland.

SIGN YOUR NAME HERE

Official Driver's License for
RICHFIELD AUTOPIA
AT Disneyland

This certifies that the undersigned has successfully passed the Safe Driver's Test for the Richfield Autopias at Disneyland.

SIGN YOUR NAME HERE

Original 1955 Autopia Licenses

Top: *September 1955 "Junior Identification Card"*
Middle: *Rare "White Castle" copy issued for only the first two weeks after Disneyland opened in July, 1955*
Bottom: *Walt Disney Productions Edition - Issued 1955 until 1960s*

Author's collection

From the November, 1955 edition of Rod & Custom Magazine...

"The (Autopia car) bodies bear a slight resemblance to the best lines of Mercedes, Maserati, Ghie and others all rolled into one. Added touches to the production models were wraparound aluminum bumpers, chromed hand rails on the cowl, a foam rubber covered dashboard, sealed beam headlights with a friction-driven generator to operate them and unique automatic braking system. The latter is a revision of the Mustang cycle brake but using wider linings and with the feature of being automatically applied when pressure is lightened on either accelerator pedal or when the outside hand brake is pulled back. The 160 lb. frame is fabricated from 2" square cast iron tubing and 1" pipe. The metal body supports are made from 16 gauge sheet stock. The entire car weighs 475 pounds dry. The spindles are cast steel and the front axel is of 1½ square tubing. The rack and pinion steering gear assembly, comparable to the type used in expensive foreign cars, has a ratio of 7 to 1.

Thirty six of the vehicles are painted in bright red two-tone 1955 automobile colors, the remaining four are black and white - official colors of the California Highway Patrol. The patrol cars are equipped with sirens and red lights and other distinctive insignia.

The police cars are not governed and can attain a speed of 25 mph as compared to the conventional cars' top speed of 11 mph. The deputies use this extra speed to enable them to unsnarl traffic jams, lend assistance to the young and sometimes bewildered rookie drivers and to sidetrack any straggling or disabled vehicles to prevent any accidents on the miniature Autobahn.

To the amazement of everyone except the far-sighted Walt Disney, these miniature hot rods are providing the biggest thrills available in Disneyland to both the young and old and the Autopia concession is proving to be the most popular attraction of the world's largest and newest amusement park."

DISNEYLAND'S MIDGET AUTOPIA

Disneyland's Autopia has always been a huge hit with young drivers since opening day in 1955, and even today no matter what time you visit the attraction, you'll find it is bustling with activity. Day or night, the air is filled with the sound of accelerating engines, squealing hot brakes, and shouts of excitement as young guests eagerly take the wheel of a stylish sports car and hit the road. Shortly after Disneyland opened, it became apparent that this attraction was a big hit and everyone wanted to ride it, not only those who took the wheel, but also those guests who were left on the side of the road wishing they, too, were tall enough to reach the gas pedal. To accommodate these younger guests, Walt soon created Junior Autopia, and on May 13, 1956, its cars took to a new track, separate from the original Autopia but complete with "booster blocks", which allowed younger drivers to reach the gas pedal just as their taller brothers and sisters could on the original Autopia.

As with the original Autopia, Junior Autopia also proved to be a big hit. However, it soon became apparent that yet another Autopia was needed, one for even smaller guests, perhaps as young as 4 years of age, and on April 23, 1957, Disneyland welcomed it's third Autopia attraction, Midget Autopia.

Featuring the smallest of the three Autopia tracks, Midget Autopia took its young yet adventurous guests on a casual drive through the "countryside" instead of California's fast-paced Freeways. Riding in cars built specifically for their smaller stature, complete with a stylish chrome Hood Rocket from the popular 1957 Chevy, the young drivers made their way along a short and winding route past landscaped hillsides before "crashing" through the doors of a small yellow barn. Unlike the Autopia and Junior Autopia cars, these smaller cars were the domain of only these youngest of kids, as they were too small for older kids and adults to fit into. Two steering wheels allowed both occupants to "drive", though the cars kept to the center of the road with the help of a center bus bar, which not only prevented any accidents, but also governed the acceleration, speed, and braking of the vehicles, much to the delight of waiting parents.

Walt Disney and his Imagineers designed and built a number of attractions specifically for the 1964 / 1965 New York World's Fair, including the now iconic "it's a small world". Walt had planned on moving the attraction to Disneyland after the World's Fair finished, so in April of 1966 he closed Midget Autopia so as to make room for "it's a small world" and its coming debut on May 28, 1966.

With the Midget Autopia attraction now dismantled and in storage, Walt, along with his brother Roy, decided to donate its 10 small cars and components to Marceline, Missouri, the small town Walt lived in from ages five to nine, and the place he credited with shaping many of his early creative thoughts.

> *"To tell the truth, more things of importance happened to me in Marceline than have happened since - or are likely to in the future. Things, I mean, like seeing my first circus parade, attending my first school, seeing my first motion*

picture. I know you'll agree with me that such childhood 'firsts' as those are of utmost importance in any human being's life." - Walt Disney - 1938

Only a few short months after it closed at Disneyland, Midget Autopia traversed a new track in Marceline's Walt Disney Municipal Park, opening there on July 4, 1966. Just as with Disneyland, the new attraction was a big hit with the young drivers of Marceline. Unfortunately, where Disneyland had the manpower, tools and expertise to maintain such an attraction, the small town of Marceline did not, and the attraction slowly fell into a state of disrepair over time. Eleven years after its arrival, the town was forced to cease its operation, and the components of Midget Autopia were tucked away into a barn, where the untended components deteriorated over time.

Today, former drivers and guests wanting to see the remainder of Disneyland's Midget Autopia can stop by the Walt Disney Hometown Museum in Marceline and see an original car on display. (As shown on the page before last.)

Photo courtesy of Peter Whitehead - Walt Disney Hometown Museum

BOB GURR AS A "DIMENSIONAL FEATURE"

"If it moves on wheels at Disneyland, I probably designed it."

- Disney Legend Bob Gurr

In 1954, Walt hired a young 22 year-old Bob Gurr to help design and build the Autopia cars for Disneyland. Favoring the sleek lines of the sports cars and airplanes of the era, Bob had developed a reputation for innovative and futuristic design and engineering while working at the Ford Motor Company, something Walt felt would complement his vision for Tomorrowland. Impressed with his work, Walt invited Bob to come to work for him at WED Enterprises, the precursor to today's Walt Disney Imagineering, and over the course of his nearly 40 year career, Bob helped develop over 100 ride vehicles that are now in use at Disney parks worldwide, including the first-of-their-kind bobsleds of the Matterhorn, the old-fashioned vehicles of Main Street, U.S.A., the sleek Disneyland Monorail, and the Doombuggies of the Haunted Mansion.

On the north side of Center Street, next to the dentist office of E.S. Bitz, D.D.S., is a window honoring Disney Legend Bob Gurr, and it reads...

"Leading the Race to the Future - Meteor Cycle Co. - Our vehicles pass the test of time - Fast, Faultless and Fadless."

What's notable about Bob's window is that it is accompanied by a hanging sign for the Meteor Cycle Co., which extends from the building façade and features an old-fashioned bicycle. Of all of the windows which honor Disney notables in the Disney theme parks around the world, this is the first window of its kind to include an accompanying "dimensional feature".

You'll sometimes read that the bicycle used on the Meteor Cycle Co. sign is Bob Gurr's childhood bike. I reached out to Bob to get his take on this, and he told me that this is actually incorrect. According to Bob, "*The bicycle was assembled from junk parts laying around the boneyard by one of the Disneyland machine shop technicians and done on his own time, not during working hours. It was his labor of love that he wanted to do for me, not part of the official window budget.*"

DECODING THE DISNEYLAND TELEGRAPH

The following article was written by Mr. George Eldridge and is reprinted with his permission. While it is available elsewhere, I wanted to include it here because it is such a great story about how a Disneyland guest came to have a permanent role in a storied Disneyland attraction quite by accident, and it leads into the following article, as well...

Several years ago I was standing at the New Orleans Train Station at Disneyland Park in Anaheim, California. Echoing in my ears was the sound of a telegraph. I, like every other ham that has visited Disneyland, listened intently to the clicks and clacks and tried to decode the message that was coming from the telegraph sounder. As a practiced CW operator on the ham bands, my first thought was that it wouldn't be too hard to decode the content. Rather than listening for tones, I'd have to think in terms of the electromagnetic sounder, which produced a "click" when energized and a "clack" when released. Thus a dit (dot) would be "click clack" and a dah (dash) would be "click (pause) clack." This sounded good in theory, but in practice it was a little more difficult than I expected. My CW gray matter just hasn't been trained for listening to the clicks and clacks in place of tones! And another thing concerned me: The rhythm of the elements wasn't quite right. In particular, I could hear a "click (pause) clack" that was much longer than the rest. At that moment I decided to return with a tape recorder and investigate further. I wasn't going to stop until I had successfully decoded the message!

A Little Detective Work

When I got home I searched the Internet for any reference to the Disneyland telegraph message. I found one reference that claimed the message was Walt Disney's inaugural speech, given at the opening of Disneyland in 1955. The telegraph message repeated every 49 seconds, however, and even at 25 words per minute it would be about 20 words, so I didn't think it could be the whole speech. As a Disneyland annual pass-holder who lives only 12 miles from the theme park, it wasn't long before I returned with a tape recorder. Actually, it was the evening of Friday, September 5, 1997. I taped about five minutes of the "code" while enduring strange looks from the other guests who were waiting for the train. I took my recorder and headed home to start the task of decoding the message.

The first thing I did was to play the tape at half speed. This made it much easier to hear the clicks and clacks. It also made it easier to hear code elements that didn't correspond to Morse code (at least the Morse code that we use as hams). I remembered seeing a table in the Callbook that listed various telegraph codes. I opened up the Callbook and, sure enough, the Continental Code (used in ham radio) was listed next to the Morse Code (used on land lines in the United States and Canada). I was surprised by the differences between the two! The letters C, F, J, L, O, P, Q, R, X, Y and Z are different. The figures and punctuation marks are different. And the elements C, O, R, Y and Z are composed of dots and spaces. T is a short dash and L is a longer dash. No wonder I was having trouble decoding the message!

At this point I decided to enlist the aid of my computer. I played the tape into my computer's sound card and digitized the audio. I could then display the waveform and see the clicks and clacks. This was much closer to Samuel F. B. Morse's original telegraph. Morse's original invention had a clockwork that moved a paper tape. The electromagnet pressed a pencil against the tape, making a sequence of dots and dashes on the moving tape. The paper tape was visually decoded to decipher the message. Telegraph operators soon found that they could decode the message just from the sounds, however, so the paper tape became an instant antique. I soon had the message decoded: "WHO COME TO THIS HAPPY PLACE, WELCOME. HERE AGE RELIVES FOND MEMORIES OF THE PAST, AND HERE YOUTH MAY SAVOR THE CHALL" The message repeated with what sounded like a splice between the "CHALL" and "WHO". Did the message start with "ALL WHO" and end with "CH", or did it start with "WHO" and end with "CHALL"? Obviously, there was a problem with the message.

A Call to the Magic Kingdom

I called Disneyland and asked to speak with someone about the damaged message. I was afraid that I might get a brush-off, but the Disney staffers were courteous and did their best to locate someone who could help me. When it became clear that no one at Disneyland could help me, they referred me to the WED studios in Burbank. I called WED and was routed to the media department - the folks there handle the sound effects at the park. I left a message explaining the damaged telegraph message. A couple of days later I received a call from media engineer Glenn Barker. Glenn explained that Disneyland is very serious about keeping things correct and was interested in getting the message fixed. He guessed that the message was accidentally truncated when it was moved from an endless loop tape player to the solid-state digital player used today. I surmised that the media engineer had listened for a repeat in the pattern and keyed in on the distinctive "LL" combination. Unfortunately, he failed to realize that the pattern "LL" occurred twice in the message.

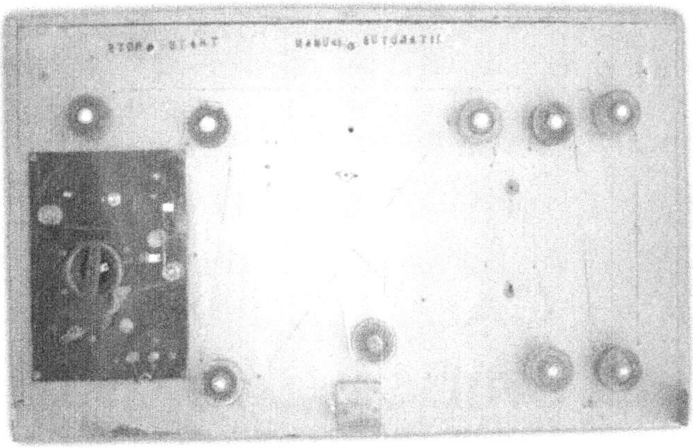

Original Frontierland RR Station Telegraph Tape Player
Photo used with permission

Glenn said he'd try to dig up the original tape and call me back. A couple of weeks later I got a call from Glenn saying he had found the original tape - but there was a problem. On the original tape the message repeats several times, but because Glenn didn't understand telegraphy, he couldn't tell where the message started or ended. I offered to decode the message and mark the beginning and end points. Glenn played the tape into my voice mail, which I downloaded onto my computer and decoded as before. I edited the sound clip so it contained just one copy of the message and played the clip into Glenn's voice mail. Glenn was able to update the digital player at the New Orleans Train Station so that it plays the correct message. He even added a pause at the end of the message to make the repeat more obvious.

It's interesting that we used modern technology to send and decode a telegraph message. I'm sure Samuel Morse never expected that someone would one day use a computer to decode a telegraph message. I had achieved my goal of decoding the message and had an interesting adventure in doing it. I hope my tale has entertained you enough that the next time you hear telegraphy you'll make an effort to decode the hidden message.

And the corrected message?...

"TO ALL WHO COME TO THIS HAPPY PLACE, WELCOME. HERE AGE RELIVES FOND MEMORIES OF THE PAST, AND HERE YOUTH MAY SAVOR THE CHALLENGE AND PROMISE OF THE FUTURE."

CALLING MR. ELDRIDGE...AGAIN!

Epcot's Spaceship Earth attraction takes guests on a journey through time as they marvel at scenes depicting the advancement of communication technology over the ages, from the invention of papyrus for written communication between men to today's digital signals transmitted between planets.

In 2008, Spaceship Earth underwent a significant reimagineering, and as part of that the Disney Imagineers wanted to represent the era of telegraphy, captured in a scene in which a telegraph operator transmits the historical news of the ceremonial driving of the Golden Spike near Promontory Summit, Utah on May 10, 1869, thus completing the Transcontinental Railroad. To "plus" the scene, the Imagineers decided to have the sound of the Morse Code being tapped out by the telegraph operator be audible to guests as they traveled by in their vehicles, and to ensure its accuracy, it was further decided that this Morse Code would be in "American Morse", or "Railroad Morse", as it was also known, as this was the type of Morse Code used in that part of the country at that point in time. However, this presented a problem when it came to finding someone today who could tap out that message, as American Morse became largely extinct in the early 1900s, being replaced by International Morse Code.

In considering their options, one of the Disney Imagineers, Glenn Barker, recalled a guest, Mr. George Eldridge, who had brought to his attention years before an error Mr. Eldridge had noticed in the Morse Code being tapped out for Walt Disney's Opening Day speech at the Disneyland Railroad New Orleans Square Station.

Realizing Mr. Eldridge could probably help the Imagineers solve this current problem, Mr. Barker contacted him and asked for his assistance. After getting up to speed on American Morse Code, Mr. Eldridge tapped out the message you hear today in the Spaceship Earth attraction, thus making him perhaps the only guest to have his work featured in an attraction in both Disneyland and Walt Disney World!

The message you hear being tapped out in the Spaceship Earth telegraphy scene...

PROMONTORY UTAH
GOLDEN SPIKE
RR CPT
USA CONNECTED

Where "RR CPT" is the Railway Telegraph abbreviation for "Railroad Complete.

Source: My interview with Mr. George Eldridge

THE DAWN REDWOOD

Standing right next to Disneyland's The Golden Horseshoe, facing toward New Orleans Square, is what is to many guests simply a tree. However, this tree is very special, as it is a rare Dawn Redwood.

During the Paleocene and Eocene periods, the Dawn Redwood, or Metasequoia, grew extensively throughout North America, with forests growing in Canada, the northern United States, and the West Coast, including within Central Oregon. Over time, however, these forests died out, leaving only fossils, and modern era experts believed the trees had been extinct for at least 1.5 million years. However, in 1943, a man by the name of Zhan Wang made an amazing discovery of a stand of unidentified trees growing in China, which, upon further analysis, turned out to be living examples of the Dawn Redwood.

Bill Evans, the man Walt Disney charged with landscaping Disneyland, was given one of four cuttings from the prized newly discovered tree, which he cultivated and ultimately planted at Disneyland, where it continues to grow today.

Note: Unlike the California Redwood, the Dawn Redwood is deciduous and loses its needles in the winter.

Big Thunder Mountain's Dietz Lantern

As you make your way through Big Thunder Mountain Railroad, you'll come to the base of a set of double stairs leading up to the loading platform. Before climbing the stairs, look to your right and you'll see on a shelf an oil lantern with the name "Dietz" emblazoned on its frosted glass. This, and two others on the attraction, are the only lanterns of their kind found within the park.

Typically, in a manner similar to the windows on Main Street, U.S.A., a name displayed such as this pays homage to an individual who played an important role within The Walt Disney Company, such as a notable animator, an innovative Imagineer, or perhaps someone who helped design and build Disneyland. However, in this case, the Disney Imagineers are paying tribute to someone outside the world of Disney with an obscure connection to the early days of Disneyland!

In 1955, when Walt was building his brand new park, he bought all of the lanterns used in Frontierland from the R. E. Dietz Lantern Company, which was founded by Robert E. Dietz.

It would be easy to assume that this lantern is then a tribute to Mr. Dietz, but that would be a bit of an overly generous honor to be bestowed upon a vendor who sold some lanterns to Walt. Instead, this is a nod by the Disney Imagineers to Alfred Clinch Dietz, Robert's cousin, who ran a General Store in San Francisco during the 1850s that provided all of the supplies the rugged forty-niners of the California Gold Rush needed to work their claims, including harnesses and saddles for their horses, bags of grain, wire, mining tools, and of course, coal oil lanterns made by the Dietz Lantern Company.

Unfortunately, the original lanterns Walt bought in 1955 were manufactured with components made of tin, which slowly wore out, thus requiring the lanterns to be replaced over time.

Original 1955 Lanterns

As guests enter Frontierland, they'll find the Pioneer Mercantile, a trading post supplying western wear, leather goods, precious stones and all kinds of Disneyland souvenirs, including Mickey Mouse ears, for those who are about to venture out yonder into the Wild West.

As you step onto the porch at the entrance of the Pioneer Mercantile, look up and you will notice a collection of lanterns hanging from a couple of large wooden beams. The red lanterns are just "modern day" decorations, but the six green lanterns hanging here are a piece of historical Disneyland, as these are the actual Deitz and Embury lanterns which the Imagineers hung in Frontierland during Disneyland's opening year in 1955. *Photos courtesy of www.WDWGuidedTours.com and Mike Grimm*

THE FUSING CAGE

As you make your way through the queue of Big Thunder Mountain Railroad in Orlando's Magic Kingdom, you'll notice the door to the "Fusing Cage" is adorned with the names of notable Disney Imagineers who contributed to the development of the attraction. Though this tribute is located in Orlando, each person listed here played an important part in creating the Disneyland we see today in Anaheim, with some having actually worked with Walt to help build his new park.

Here's a short bio for each...

Little Big Gibson - Blaine Gibson

In addition to providing animation for early Disney classic films, including Fantasia, Peter Pan and Sleeping Beauty, Blaine Gibson created hundreds of accurately detailed sculptures for such attractions as Great Moments with Mr. Lincoln, the Haunted Mansion, Pirates of the Caribbean and more. Perhaps his most famous work is of the bronze statue "Partners", which depicts Walt and Mickey standing hand in hand and can be found in the hub of Disney theme parks around the world.

Jolley the Kid - Bob Jolley

As Field Art Director, Bob Jolley used his Imagineering talents to combine Big Thunder Mountain Railroad's shiny new technology with its authentic mining past. Recognized as an expert in show finishes and skilled in the craft of aging story elements, he blended the new and old together to give the entire attraction the rustic historic look we see today.

Buckaroo Burke - Pat Burke

Pat Burke was the WDI Imagineer responsible for designing many of the attractions found throughout Disney theme parks worldwide, including four Big Thunder Mountains, four Indiana Jones, three Jungle Cruises and the original Splash Mountain. It is commonly known among guests that the authentic mining equipment found throughout the different Big Thunder Mountain attractions came from many different locations across the United States, and Pat Burke was the man who was responsible for discovering it all and bringing it to the parks.

Calamity Clem - Clem Hall

Clem Hall was a concept artist responsible for creating conceptual artwork for numerous Disneyland and Walt Disney World attractions, including Big Thunder Mountain Railroad.

Skittish Skip - Skip Lange

Skip Lange of Walt Disney Imagineering was responsible for designing the unique mountain landscape of Disneyland's Big Thunder Mountain Railroad, fashioning the look after the "hoodoos" found in Bryce Canyon National Park in Utah. He would go on to design the rockwork for every Big Thunder Mountain Railroad attraction found in Disney theme parks worldwide.

Wild Wolf Joerger - Fred Joerger

An important part of every attraction's development is the crafting of miniature 3-D models which represent how the attraction will look when finished. Fred Joerger, in addition to crafting models for early Disney movie sets and "most everything at Disneyland", was known as the "resident rock expert" because of his expertise in designing and crafting the large realistic stonework found throughout Disneyland and Walt Disney World, including the stonework found at the Jungle Cruise, Pirates of the Caribbean and Big Thunder Mountain Railroad.

Matchstick Marc - Marc Davis

This is a tribute to a Disney Legend and one of Disney's "Nine Old Men" of animation, Marc Davis. In addition to animating such classic Disney characters as Cinderella, Snow White, Tinker Bell, Cruella De Vil, Brer Rabbit, Bambi, Alice and others, Mr. Davis played an important role in the development of characters for many of your favorite attractions, including Pirates of the Caribbean, The Jungle Cruise, "it's a small world", The Country Bear Jamboree, the Haunted Mansion, The Enchanted Tiki Room and more. This isn't the only homage to Marc Davis in the park, as guests will also find a tombstone at the Haunted Mansion which reads...

In Memory Of
Our Patriarch
Dear Departed
Grandpa
Marc

Mama Hutchinson - Helena Hutchinson

Helena Hutchinson practiced her craft in the Figure Finishing department at Walt Disney Imagineering, which was responsible for adorning the multitude of characters that appeared in the parks, be they birds, goats, buffaloes, tigers, skeletons or human figures, in everything from fur and paint to feathers and costumes. As an expert in working with fur, she finished the animals found throughout Big Thunder Mountain Railroad.

Mrs. Potts' Cold Handle Sad Iron

While visiting Silver Spurs Supplies in Frontierland, you'll notice hanging on the wall a small framed advertisement for Mrs. Potts' Cold Handle Sad Iron. One would think this is just a vintage ad placed as a simple story element, or perhaps a clever reference to the Mrs. Potts character in Disney's animated movie, *Beauty and the Beast.* However, it is instead a homage by the Imagineers to an enterprising young woman who, as a 19 year-old in 1869, invented a revolutionary clothes iron that would take the frontier, and the world, by storm.

In the mid-1800s, "Sad" was an old English word meaning heavy, solid, or dense, and as such, clothes irons were referred to as "sad irons", since, being made of solid cast iron, they would weigh anywhere from five to ten pounds. Because this was prior to the widespread use of electricity in the home, these heavy irons were heated atop a woodburning stove, and being cast as a single unit, the entire piece, including the iron handle, would get blistering hot, thus requiring the user to wrap the handle in a thick cloth or mitt so as to use it without blistering their fingers. In a world dominated by businessmen, young Mary Florence Potts had a better idea...*What if irons were made with a wooden handle, one which would not conduct heat?* And with that, a revolution was born!

Soon, Mrs. Potts had a patent for her idea and the American Machine Company of Philadelphia was producing thousands of irons every day, each including a detachable curved wooden handle, a set of three different sized irons, and a metal trivet upon which to rest the iron when not in use.

Burned fingers were a thing of the past on the frontier and across the globe, and Mrs. Potts' iron went on to become a standard household item, while she went on to become a very successful and well respected "inventress", lecturer, and businesswoman, not to mention the subject of a small homage hidden in Silver Spurs Supplies in Disneyland's Frontierland.

A Dark Ride Challenge

As you glide, spin or careen your way through any of Disneyland's classic "dark rides", the story elements illuminated in black light pop with vivid color, adding a dramatic sense to each story. It's one of the key elements which make them such beloved and classic attractions. Have you ever wondered about the process the Disney Imagineers use to paint these unique black-lit scenes and the challenges they face in doing so? 30 year Imagineer Cindy Bothner explains what's involved...

"Black light painting is a very different animal, because you are basically painting with light. Depending on the amount of regular acrylic paint you mix in with the black colors, you can get a wide variety of light effects. You have to learn to control the amount of black light pigment you use so that everything does not end up popping at the same time. We wanted to avoid giving it the look of a carnival ride. We had to learn to mix our paints so that the piece we were painting looked the same under white light as it did under black light, only with a little more pop to it.

It was very challenging at first. An individual scene was constructed and black dubetyne was put up as a tent. We would paint it under black light in there. Once the scene was finished, a buy-off was scheduled and it was either approved or required changes were made."

FUR THE BIRDS, TUPPENCE A BAG

Opening in June of 1963, Walt Disney's Enchanted Tiki Room was the first attraction to include Walt's new Audio-Animatronic technology, allowing a cast of over 150 talking, singing and dancing birds to entertain guests in a Polynesian setting.

Photo courtesy of Dave Drumheller

Have you ever wondered how Disneyland's Figure Finishing Department adorned all the Audio-Animatronic birds in their bright plumage such that they could move and still appear as real birds? 30 year Imagineer Cindy Bothner explains the process in this interview, which is reprinted here with her kind permission...

"Fur and feathering a Tiki Bird is quite involved. If I remember correctly, it takes about 36 hours, maybe less after you get the hang of it. First, you are given a fiberglass and kydex (an alternate to leather) bird body. A pattern is made of muslin for the fur cloth, or bird fur. The pattern has to allow for the movement of the head, but still be snug enough so as not to bunch up and look fake. Very tricky!

You also have to craft a spandex collar that is glued to the neck opening, which keeps the bird fur from folding into the neck area when the bird moves. You then cut out the fur cloth according to the pattern. Before gluing it on, you paint the cloth the desired colors, which are air-brushed on with

permanent ink. The face and feet are then painted with water-based acrylics. After the painting, you glue on the fur cloth and then feather the wings and tail. This is done in a specific pattern using pre-selected feathers that are trimmed just right.
We also had to decorate the cages for the Tiki Room. We were given a cage fabricated from metal tubing. We applied Bondo to the tubing (Bondo could easily be carved to look like wood), and then painted and decorated the cages.

We had a wonderful teacher for the whole Tiki project in Leota Thomas. Leota and Harriet Burns were the Imagineers who furred and feathered the original Tiki Birds for Disneyland, and then later for Walt Disney World.

Leota was originally from the Walt Disney Studios, where she had worked in the Ink & Paint Department. She came over to WED when Disney first started the company. Without this wonderful lady teaching us the intricacies of the Tiki Birds, it would have been very time-consuming to figure out the exact method. She also taught us the use of 'Animal Vinyl Paint', which was used on the flexible bodies of the Animatronic figures, animal and human, as well as the Elephants, Hippos and others in the Jungle Cruise. The paint was actually a liquid form of the skin itself."

THE INSPIRATION FOR TODAY'S AUDIO-ANIMATRONICS

A Bontems Mechanical Bird

Beginning with the opening of Walt Disney's Enchanted Tiki Room in Disneyland in June of 1963, and followed by the amazing first-of-its-kind display of a standing and speaking President Lincoln at the 1964 / 1965 New York World's Fair, Disney's Audio-Animatronics technology has always played an important role in entertaining, informing, amusing and even frightening guests as they enjoy the show that plays at Disney theme parks around the world each and every day.

Be it "Chef Remy", a small yet personable rat in Epcot, a towering fire-breathing dragon in Fantasmic!, or even the many rascals, scoundrels, villains and knaves found in the different Pirates of the Caribbean attractions across the globe, all of these "characters" are a result of a single moment of inspiration, which Walt drew from a small gilded birdcage he spotted in an antiques shop while on vacation in New Orleans.

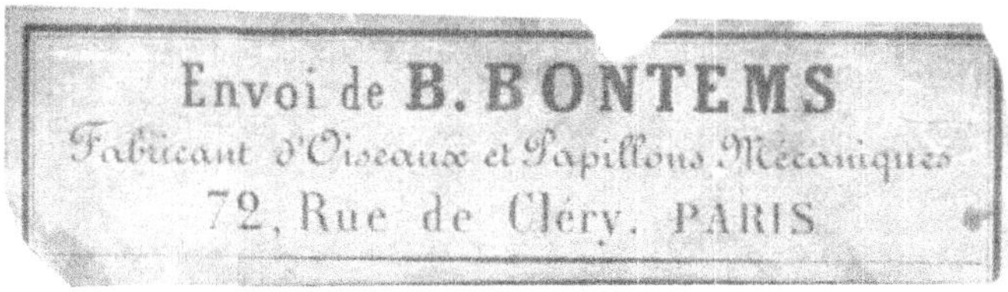

Inside this golden birdcage was a tiny feathered bird, which moved and sang as though alive through the creative use of tiny gears and bellows. A form of entertainment in the late 19th century, it was manufactured by B. Bontems, a small company located at 72, Rue de Clery, Paris and known as a "Manufacturer of Birds and Butterflies Machine Heads." The model Walt found was manufactured as early as 1850.

Seeing the small bird within the cage "perform", Walt was intrigued by how the mechanism located within the base of the cage worked to bring the small bird to life, and he pondered how he might be able to expand upon that technology to bring characters, animals and even humans to "life" within his new theme park. He purchased the antique birdcage and gave it to Roger Broggie, who in turn provided it to Wathel Rogers. Walt had charged Wathel and Fred Joerger to create architectural models for Disneyland's upcoming construction, so Wathel was just the person to decipher the small and intricate details of this intriguing antique.

Discovering a system of gears, springs and bellows, Wathel and Roger explained how it all worked to Walt, who, in seeing the possibilities, charged Roger and his team with developing and improving upon the concept to ultimately create the concept of Audio-Animatronics.

"Just as we had to learn to make our animated cartoons talk, we had to find a way to make these characters talk, too. Now, to accomplish this, we created a new type of animation. So new that we had to invent a new name for it...Audio-Animatronics."

- Walt Disney

Walt and his team of Imagineers began to explore applying this new technology to various story elements within Disneyland, ultimately leading to the opening of the innovative Walt Disney's Enchanted Tiki Room attraction in June of 1963. About this time, Walt was asked to develop some attractions for the 1964 / 1965 New York World's Fair. Seeing this as an opportunity to showcase the new Audio-Animatronics technology, he set out to move beyond what had been created so far and began developing a full size human figure in the form of Abraham Lincoln. Appearing in the Great Moments with Mr. Lincoln attraction in the Illinois pavilion at the World's Fair, Walt's new Audio-Animatronic figure of America's 16th President greeted guests while seated in a chair, but soon rose to his feet and began delivering moments from some of his more notable speeches. Having seen nothing like it ever before, audiences were amazed at the lifelike appearance of the figure and its ability to stand up from a chair and speak.

"...the final result is so lifelike, you may find it hard to believe."

- Walt Disney

In addition to the Great Moments with Mr. Lincoln attraction, Walt and his team also created three other attractions for the fair, including "it's a small world", The Ford Magic Skyway and the General Electric Carousel of Progress, all of which used the new Audio-Animatronic technology. Today, this technology has been honed to create hundreds of lifelike characters, which guests enjoy every day at Disney theme parks around the world.

An Homage of a Different Feather

It's interesting to note that the Imagineers pay homage to this small birdcage and its important role in the history of The Walt Disney Company in a small scene within Disneyland. If guests make their way to the Fairy Tale Treasures gift shop in Disneyland's Fantasy Faire, they'll find Figaro, the cat belonging to Geppetto the woodcarver, who created Pinocchio in Disney's 1940 animated film by the same name, lying high on an outdoor windowsill. In this scene created by the Imagineers, Figaro is attempting to take a catnap, but a small bird in a cage next to him keeps him awake with its cheerful chirping. While not looking anything like the small feathered mechanical bird Walt found in the antique store, the Imagineers programmed this modern day bird with the very same movements as the antique bird, with a swivel of its head, a chirp from its beak and an occasional twitch of its tail feathers.

Photo courtesy of www.Disneygeek.com

FIGARO MAKES AN "EXIT"

In the entry way of Disneyland's Red Rose Taverne in Fantasyland is a Disneyland secret that is familiar to some guests. Placed above two entry way doors is an "Exit" sign. The sign itself is nothing out of the ordinary, but it's placement is, as it is immediately obvious that it is a bit off center from where a sign such as this is usually located, that being in the *middle* above the two doors. In a bit of whimsy, the Disney Imagineers have painted Sultan, a character from Disney's animated hit Beauty and the Beast, as pulling on a rope attached to the sign in an effort to pull it back into place. However, Sultan has not always been the character depicted here. The Red Rose Taverne used to be the Village Haus restaurant, and the character originally depicted as tugging on the sign was not Sultan, but instead Figaro, Geppetto's cat. The following is the first-ever complete story of how Figaro came to be painted here, as shared with me by Disney Imagineer Terry Peterson...

The story of the Figaro gag is this: It was 1983, and after painting tons of art that would adorn the walls of the Fantasyland rides as well as the Village Haus restaurant, I and another colleague started the location work of tying in the murals with the 3D elements. After painting the dwarves' cottage and other elements in the Pinocchio load/unload, I was assigned the touch-up and tie-in of my murals going into the restaurant. I noticed that the exit sign was off center, and I knew it was because there was a structural element on center that would not accommodate the recess necessary for the sign housing. Having established a comfortable relationship with the great art director Tony Baxter, I decided to take a chance and paint Figaro starting to pull the sign to its proper spot and giving a wink to those "in" on the joke. When Tony came in the next day I pulled him aside and said, "Look, I did something on my own and if you hate it, I can make it go away in five minutes - it's only paint." He took one look and after figuring what must have happened he said, "NO! I love it, leave it!" Funny enough, the myth surrounding it lived on without me but when the restaurant was duplicated in Paris, (where I contributed much work, but not this) an artist rendered Figaro leaning on the properly placed exit sign, winking and giving the thumbs up. Talk about an inside joke. I loved it!"

Photos courtesy of Terry Peterson

A Backwards Sleeping Beauty Castle?

1953 Model by Marvin Davis and Fred Joerger

Here's an in-depth detail with a bit of a twist...or shall we say "turn"?

In 1953, Disney Legend and Imagineer Herb Ryman worked with Walt to begin sketching out Walt's vision for his new park, Disneyland. Amidst all the different lands, stories and attractions, Walt knew he wanted a commanding icon, one which would not only provide a visible "anchor" for guests as they navigated their way about, but also one which would encapsulate all the fantasy, magic, adventure and memories of Disneyland.

Using elements of Neuschwanstein Castle in Bavaria, Germany as his inspiration, Herb drew up a vision for the castle, with imposing walls, towering keeps and colorful flags.

Once the initial design of Sleeping Beauty Castle had been honed, the design task was handed over to Imagineer and future Disney Legend Fred Joerger, who would create a 3-D model of the castle so the Imagineering team could "see" it in real life. Newly hired in 1953, Fred would go on to create models for countless Disney movies, Animatronic figures, attractions, Disneyland structures and more. In fact, Disney Legend Harriet Burns once said, "*Most anything at Disneyland, Fred created as a model first.*"

Back of Sleeping Beauty Castle Today

Using his impressive artistic skills, Fred created a few different versions of the castle, changing different design elements with each revision. During one review session, Herb Ryman felt something wasn't quite right. According to Herb...

"*One thing that he (Walt) insisted upon was that there be a very, very conspicuous castle, because the castle is going to be the symbol of this whole place. Fred Joerger had done a beautiful model of this castle. When I saw it I said, 'I don't like it.' So I took a look at the castle model, grabbed a hold of the upper portion of the model, and turned it around so that the back of the upper portion now faced the front. 'Dick said, 'Now, Herbie, quit playing with it. Put it back. He said 'Walt's going to be here any minute, and Walt won't like it. Turn it around. Put it back.'*"

The next thing you know, Walt walked in. Herb hadn't had a chance to turn the castle back around, so everyone was concerned Walt would be upset with the new look. To the contrary, however. He thought it looked great.

"Walt said, 'Oh, I like that a lot better.' So then Marvin and Dick began to like it a lot better. It was always a confused point with us, but today (the front) is facing inside."

So the front of Sleeping Beauty Castle you see today was originally supposed to be the back!

Take a look at the castle model created in 1953 by Marvin Davis and Fred Joerger before Sleeping Beauty Castle was constructed, and see how the appearance of the front of the model more closely resembles the back of the Sleeping Beauty Castle you see in the park today.

Sleeping Beauty Castle Weenie

In every Disney theme park you'll find a visual "weenie", a dominant park icon which draws guests further into the park. For Disneyland, Sleeping Beauty Castle beckons guests down Main Street, U.S.A. for a day of magic and memories. For the Magic Kingdom, it's Cinderella Castle, for Epcot it's Spaceship Earth and for Disney's Animal Kingdom, it's the Tree of Life.

Using a visual "weenie" to draw in guests was a concept adopted by Walt...

"What you need is a weenie, which says to people 'come this way.' People won't go down a long corridor unless there's something promising at the end. You have to have something that beckons them to 'walk this way.'" - Walt Disney

As Walt designed and built Disneyland, many of the ideas he implemented in his new park were inspired by events from his past; a small mechanical bird discovered in an antique shop in New Orleans provided the inspiration for what would become Audio-Animatronics and Walt Disney's Enchanted Tiki Room, while Marceline, Missouri was the inspiration for Main Street, U.S.A., and of course, a Merry-Go-Round at Griffith Park was the inspiration for Disneyland itself. Walt was always absorbing inspiration throughout his life. There is a story about Walt getting the idea for weenies from when his dog would follow him around whenever he had hot dogs or baloney in his coat pocket, but this strikes me as a bit mundane for a man of Walt's genius. Perhaps...just perhaps...Walt's inspiration for his theme park weenies came from one of the many inspirations he is known to have drawn from his trips to France, including one to Paris in June of 1949.

In 1853, Napoleon III directed Georges Eugene Haussmann to reconstruct much of Paris by demolishing its dark and cramped housing along narrow winding streets and replace it with wide boulevards, avenues and open spaces which would let in both sunlight and air. As part of this charge, Haussmann constructed inviting boulevards to connect the different parts of the city, many of which he purposely aligned so that a grand monument, such as the Pantheon, Arc de Triomphe or Opera Palais Garnier, would provide a focal point in the distance. During his lifetime, Walt made a number of trips to Paris, including during his service with the Red Cross as an ambulance driver in 1918, as well as while on a family vacation during 1949, and perhaps it was during one of these visits that Walt drew inspiration from Haussman's open-flowing boulevards with grand focal points for use with his upcoming park, Disneyland.

THE CAPITOL OF DISNEYLAND

In the foyer of Disneyland's *The Great Moments with Mr. Lincoln* attraction, guests will notice a large and magnificently detailed model of our National Capitol Building. Many guests incorrectly assume this was designed and built by Disney Imagineers for *The Great Moments with Mr. Lincoln* attraction, but it actually has a history which pre-dates Disneyland by more than 20 years. What follows here is *the first-ever published account* of how this model was created, as well as how Walt came to own it.

Made of Caenstone, this highly detailed model was sculpted by Mr. George H. Lloyd. Born in March, 1879 in Llanelly, South Wales, Mr. Lloyd learned the skills of stone sculpting and engraving as a young man from his father before immigrating to Canada via steamship in 1907, eventually settling in Ottawa. Highly skilled at the art, he practiced his trade on such stately buildings as the Cathedral of St. John the Devine and The Rockefeller Church, both in New York, McGill University in Montreal, and the Canadian Parliament Building in Ottawa, Canada. Mr. Lloyd stated the inspiration for creating his model of the U.S. Capitol Building "*...came to me in 1918 when I saw a picture of the capitol in a Philadelphia paper. I didn't have time to work on the model until the depression when I was out of work.*"

In 1932, only a few years after Mickey Mouse made his debut in Steamboat Willie and 23 years before Disneyland opened, 53 year-old Mr. Lloyd journeyed to Washington D.C. to meet with the Capitol's architect, Mr. David Lynn, where he explained his intent to carve an intricate miniature reproduction of the building out of Caenstone, a fine-grained limestone quarried from the Caen area of Normandy, France. Impressed by Mr. Lloyd's plans, Mr. Lynn graciously supplied him with pictures, drawings and blueprints, which would not only make the model easier to sculpt, but would ensure its accuracy, as well. With these materials in hand, Mr. Lloyd began the slow and deliberate task of hand-carving over 500 pieces out of stone, a process of intricate craftsmanship which would require many 16 hour days over the course of over three and a half years to finish, resulting in the magnificent structure we see today.

Cathedral of St. John the Devine - New York

In 1940, nearly five years after he had finished, Mr. Lloyd began to tour the country while displaying his Capitol model in the department stores of cities large and small, including Chicago, Memphis, Portland, Salt Lake City, San Francisco and Los Angeles, among others. In this era, during the remainder of

Photo courtesy of Jordan Sallis
Mr. Lloyd's great, great, great niece

the Great Depression and before the advent of widespread television, a patriotic and notable achievement such as this would be a form of quality entertainment, and people would journey from miles around to come see it. Eventually, millions of Americans did come to view its stately beauty, and one of those was Walt Disney himself. Being both patriotic and a fan of detailed miniatures, Walt engaged in correspondence with Mr. Lloyd about buying his model with the intention of putting it on display near the entrance of a new land he was adding to Disneyland, called "Liberty Street".

On October 18, 1955, Mr. Lloyd was displaying his model in Robinson's Department Store in Southern Los Angeles and wrote to Walt to see if "*...you are still interested in my replica of the National Capital*".(sic) Walt and Mr. Lloyd agreed to terms, and the following Monday, October 24, 1955, Walt had the U.S. Capitol Building model he wanted for "Liberty Street" in the Studio.

Mr. Lloyd would later write to his family...

Photo courtesy of Jordan Sallis

"I displayed my work in Los Angeles...and sold it to a well known motion picture man named Walt Disney and it will be on permanent display at his wonderful exhibition grounds at Los Angeles."

Unfortunately, Liberty Street was never completed, yet the U.S. Capitol Building model was eventually displayed with the *Great Moments with Mr. Lincoln* attraction beginning in 1965, where it resides today, and its stately beauty has been enjoyed by millions of guests from around the world ever since.

Mr. Lloyd passed away in Palo Alto, California in May, 1962 at the age of 82.

An extremely rare June, 1944 brochure distributed by Lowenstein's Department Store in Memphis, TN.
Author's Collection

Mr. Lloyd's words from his WWII era promotional brochure titled, "George H. Lloyd's Hand Carved Caenstone Model of Our National Capitol"...

"I made up my mind to some day carve a model from stone and accordingly went to Washington D. C. where I met Mr. David Lynn, the Capitol architect, who treated me with great kindness. I explained my project and to my great delight, Mr. Lynn made available to me numerous photographs, drawings and blueprints that made the task much easier and insured accuracy. It has taken me 3 1/2 years to complete my model but I have enjoyed every minute of it, and feel that many thousands of people who have perhaps never visited the Capitol will look with interest and pleasure at this work."

Note: In writing this book, I wondered about the history of the miniature hand carved stone model of the U.S. Capitol Building on display within the Great Moments with Mr. Lincoln attraction, as well as the man who created it. Little to nothing about either was available anywhere, and the plaque affixed to the model at Disneyland offers only a small amount of information. I turned to the web to begin my research and there I found an image of an original World War II era brochure, which was for sale on eBay. Issued by Lowenstein's Department Store in Memphis, Tennessee, it promoted the display of the U.S. Capitol model by Mr. Lloyd in their store in June of 1944. That in itself was interesting, but even more so was the first-ever photo I had seen of Mr. Lloyd. Not only of Mr. Lloyd, but of Mr. Lloyd standing next to the very U.S. Capitol Building model now at Disneyland. This was truly a rare document tied to the history of Disneyland! I placed my bid and then began the wait for the auction to end. Would other people know the significance of this item? Would most people assume it's just an old brochure and overlook it? Does anyone even know who George H. Lloyd is? Thankfully, the auction ended and I was the sole bidder. The price I paid...$5.50.

As I had hoped, upon its receipt the brochure offered up a great deal of all new information about Mr. Lloyd, as well as additional clues to follow as part of my research. I am happy to share this with you in what is the *first-ever publication of this information and photos of Mr. Lloyd in any Disney-related content.*

Lastly, inside the brochure is a hand stamped address for Mr. Lloyd which reads...

GEORGE LLOYD
30 Irving Street
SAN FRANCISCO 22, CALIF.

Note: *I would like to recognize the contribution of Ms. Jordan Sallis, who, along with her grandfather, Brian Hillman, generously shared information and photos which greatly contributed to this story about the Capitol of Disneyland.*

PUBLISHING WALT'S LOVE OF MODEL RAILROADING

Walt during a little publicized trip to the Chingford Model Railroad in Ridgeway Park, London, July 12, 1952

During the mid-1950s through mid-1960s, there were a small number of railfan magazines that published a handful of articles about such things as Walt Disney's love of trains, the steam trains of Disneyland, and the personal "backyard" railroads of such Disney artists and Imagineers as Ollie Johnston, Dick Bagley and Ward Kimball. Above, Walt is showing off the inaugural May - June, 1952 edition of *The Miniature Locomotive* magazine to new friends in London, England, which features a photo of Walt aboard his Lilly Belle steam engine on the front cover and an article inside written by Roger Broggie about Walt's Carolwood Pacific Railroad in the backyard of his Holmby Hills home.

Now over 60 years old, these obscure magazine articles are rarely, if ever, seen by Disney fans. However, the article on the following page is a profile of Ward Kimball, who helped Walt design the steam engines of Disneyland, among many other contributions, and it appeared in the April, 1965 issue of Railroad Magazine. - *Permission courtesy of White River Productions*

WARD KIMBALL
INTERESTING RAILFANS NO. 28

Ward Kimball and Walt Disney Aboard the Emma Nevada

The following is a profile of Ward Kimball, as it appeared in the April, 1965 issue of Railroad Magazine.

Ward Kimball is the most versatile railfan we have ever known. He invented a talking cricket, coached a chorus of singing crows, and plotted a trip to the moon - all in movie cartoons. He by-lined a book that is probably banned by every school and public library in the country. He is a railroad president and amateur astronomer. He collects vintage automobiles and other Americana, plays the trombone, and is a licensed airplane pilot.

Said Ralph J. Gleason, columnist for the San Francisco Chronicle: "Ward Kimball is a short, slight man with a face like an old-time vaudeville comic. He slaves for the big money in the Disney factories in Lotusland and for ten years or so, in between building a railroad in his back yard, he has operated a Dixieland band."

Another columnist, Jim Davis, wrote in The Parsons (Kan.) Sun: "When Ward Kimball was a five-year old, he played here in the junk locomotives of a Katy Railroad graveyard. As a result, he became a railroad buff who now has three antique Baldwin locomotives in his back yard. He also grew up to be a movie director, band leader, and author."

Two important events happened in 1914: (a) Ward Kimball was born at Minneapolis on March 14th and (b) an Austrian archduke was assassinated June 28th. The world has not been the same ever since.

On approximately the same date as the Battle of St. Mihiel in France, the subject of this sketch, then four years old, touched a locomotive for the first time, the engine being a 4-4-0 and the place being the Frisco depot at Parsons. "Frequent trips to the Parsons waterworks," Ward recalls, "where the Katy Flyer used to roar around the curve with much smoke and whistling, also were a contributing factor to my early love of railroads."

Later, back in Minneapolis and aged seven, he started on a collecting spree that he'll probably never outgrow: Cigar bands, streetcar transfers, and tin toy trolleys. (What was there about Minneapolis that gave residents the trolley bug? Frank P. Donovan, No 19 in our *Interesting Railfans* series, chartered a Minneapolis trolley for his wedding party and wrote transit articles for *Railroad Magazine.*)

Luckily, Ward had other interests. He took to drawing steam locomotives and he fell for a correspondence course in cartooning. In due time he enrolled at Stanford U. but didn't care much for college. Someone has said that "College is the place where pebbles are polished and diamonds are dimmed." Ward avoided both possibilities by winning a scholarship to the Santa Barbara Art School, quitting Stanford, and studying art.

After two years of painting trees, barns, and nudes, the lad decided he was pretty good. He was then twenty. Taking his nerve into both hands, he asked Walt Disney for a job. Disney had recently opened a studio to make Mickey Mouse cartoons for the movies and he needed animators. He looked at Ward's stuff and said, "You start here tomorrow morning at nine."

Ward was elated. He was then the youngest animator on Disney's staff. An animator, in case you didn't know, is one of the artists who draw the sequence of pictures that, when photographed and flashed on a screen, make a cartoon *move.* After doing this work for some time and occasionally writing scripts, Ward was promoted to the job of designing and directing short movie cartoons. One of these, *Toot, Whistle, Plunk and Boom*, won an Academy Award. Today he is a top animation supervisor on the Disney totem pole.

"This wonderful world of cartoons and live action," says Ward, "has never seemed to me like hard work. I love it."

When Disney embarked on television programs, our No. 28 Railfan was put in charge of *Tomorrowland* segments, including the space travel series, one of which won a TV Emmy Award. And when that fabulous amusement resort known as Disneyland was being planned, Ward served as railroad technical advisor, seeing that everything on the Disneyland Railroad was as authentic as possible. For reference material, he used his large collection of old railbooks and files of *Railroad Magazine.*

"It thrilled me," he recalls, "to watch all this wonderful equipment come to life and made me feel rather important to be part of the planning."

In the late '30's, with the economic independence of a steady, well-paying job, he began building old-time railroad models in ¼" scale as a hobby. His layout was pre-1890. No kits - everything built from scratch. He put in week-ends tracking down equipment, measuring, and drawing.

In 1934 he began dating a personable young blonde named Betty Lawyer, a color consultant at Disney's, and he married her in '36. Ward spent many *daylight* hours of his honeymoon on detailed drawings of Virginia & Truckee equipment. (Betty must have *loved* that!) Today, in spite of all this, they have two daughters, Kelly, 25, and Chloe, 18, and a son John, 23, as well as a granddaughter.

Ward's Grizzly Flats Railroad

We asked Ward about the Grizzly Flats Railroad that operates on the three-acre "back-yard" of the Kimball home on a quiet, tree-lined street at 8910 Ardendale Avenue, San Gabriel, Calif. Apparently it all started with the news that the Southern Pacific's narrow-gage at Keeler, Calif., was going to burn up its antique coaches.

"Betty and I rushed up there," he says, "and found that they wanted only $50 for an old coach. So we bought one, with the idea of turning it into a railroad museum behind the house, and we picked up enough 35-pound rail to rest it on."

"My original idea for a railroad museum was expanded when I learned that the Nevada Central, another narrow-gage line, was planning to sell its old steam engines to Japan for scrap. I purchased one of them, the *Emma Nevada*, for a mere $400."

She was No. 2, a Mogul, the last motive power to run on the NC, her final job having been hauling flatcars with scrap rail to Battle Mount, Nev. Baldwin had built her in 1881, construction number 5575; cylinders 13 x 18", weight 44,000 pounds, drivers 41" in diameter, and wheelbase 17'1".

The freight bill for hauling her to Los Angeles in a gondola was $450. Before being unloaded, she was given a rigid inspection in the SP shops. They checked her injectors, lubricators, and 8" air pump, and set the pops at 100 pounds, instead of 135, for reasons of safety. A truck then moved her to the Kimball homestead.

More track had to be laid. Track-laying is not a one-man job. But Ward Kimball was foxy. He'd read in a Mark Twain book how Tom Sawyer was given the irksome task of whitewashing a long fence. Instead of doing the job himself, Tom convinced the boys of the neighborhood that they could have fun by helping him - and they fell for his "line." By volunteer help, the fence was whitewashed with very little muscular effort on Tom's part. What Ward Kimball did, conniving with Betty, was to throw periodic tracklaying barbecues to induce friends and neighbors to assist. It worked. Today, the Grizzly Flats boasts 950 feet of "main line," thanks partly to outsiders.

"In those days," Ward tells us, "San Gabriel was largely citrus-ranch country. Some of the neighboring farmers used to stand in front of our home and wonder what was going on back there. It must have been strange for them to watch puffing steam engines move back and forth behind the house, apparently with no place to go.

"Betty and I would invite them onto our property to enjoy what was going on. For many years the Grizzly Flats has been the scene of happy gatherings of railroad buffs, women's clubs, model fans, youth groups, school classes, and lovers of Americana in general.

Meanwhile, the 2-6-0 had to be put into operating condition. There were tedious weeks of cleaning and scraping with putty knives and caustic soda. Layers of old paint were removed from both engine and tender. When the original layer was reached, care was taken to measure all lettering and striping, and the quaint decorations were recorded on tracing paper, so as to duplicate the original exactly in the final painting.

The tender tank was sand-blasted to remove all rust, and was red-leaded. Everything cleaned on the loco also was given a protective coast of red lead. But a disheartening discovery was the finding of dry rot in the oak tender frame. This necessitated complete rebuilding of that frame, after the old one has been measured accurately. It was a long and painstaking job.

Then the well-pitted throttle valve had to be ground to insure a tight seat, and a new throttle with new packing was put into place. The broken reverse lever spring was replaced, new running boards were installed, and a new 5-foot pilot was built from old SP narrow-gage blueprints. Brass flag-holders, acorn trims, and grab railings were added.

One of the many volunteer helpers was Gerald M. Best (No. 16 in our *Interesting Railfans* series), who supplied a genuine old Baldwin oilburning headlight from a Carson & Colorado engine. Atop the sandbox was attached a quaint bronze American eagle in full flight. The old wooden cab required a maximum of bracing and refitting, a roof canvas was tacked into place, and ruby red windows etched with flowers were installed.

Next came the relatively easy paint job - three coats: engine and tender wheels vermillion, striped in gold leaf; pilot headlight domes deep carmine red, also trimmed with gold leaf; cylinders and steam chest deep green and vermillion with gold-leaf floral designs; cab olive green and Venetian red, and the undercarriage and valve motion black and red. Ward himself painted nostalgic pictures on the headlight.

The tender is black, trimmed with carmine, green, and orange, and lettered *Grizzly Flats R.R.* A bit of sentiment was added by glueing pin-up girls of the '90's above the windows inside the cab. Finally, the coach was finished in gaudy canary yellow with apple-green letter boards, maroon-trimmed windows, and gold filigree. What a riot of color!

But those jobs were little more than a beginning. Other equipment was acquired, structures were built. As Ward says: "Back-yard railroading is like painting the Brooklyn Bridge. You start working from one end to the other, and then you begin all over again."

Today, alone or in groups, visitors are welcomed to the Grizzly Flats Railroad. They ride the train, gape at the 1900-model windmill, gaze up admiringly at the 7,200-gallon water tower, and browse through the 1856 vintage wooden depot.

This depot, gaily painted red and orange, is authentic in every detail. Actually, Ward designed it for a Disney film and later salvaged it from a set at the Disney studios. It now houses one of the nation's finest displays of railroadiana - buttons from passenger trainmen's uniforms, switch locks and keys, old dining-car menus, passes, tickets, posters, lanterns, watches, locomotive bells and headlights, and antique toy trains.

Aside from his railroad items, Ward has other Americana. For example: a wooden "gingerbread" doll house, made about 1890, and dolls dating back to the 1850's, and character toys from the 1920's representing celebrities of their day.

Down at the south end of the yard you can see the enginehouse, also built by ward with friends' help. Inside stand the *Emma Nevada*, that 20-ton coalburner, and coach No. 5, built in 1873, the SP's last narrow-gage passenger car and two sugar-plantation steam engines from Hawaii: the Chloe, which Ward acquired in 1948 and named for his younger daughter, and the Olomana (Big Noise), owned by "Jerry" Best.

Guarding the grade crossing near the family garage is the Pennsy-type watchman's shanty of the 1870's, and beside the depot you can't miss the big, old hand-operated target-stub switch, a V&T relic.

Among other equipment is a 40-foot boxcar, a 40-foot side-door caboose from the old Pacific Coast Railway, and a 3-foot-gate handcar from the same line. Most active piece of equipment is a Colorado & Southern push car, which is used to haul rails and ties. A wooden baggage truck came from the now-extinct Tonopah & Tidewater.

The Grizzly Flats Railroad has been featured in countless newspaper and magazine write-ups, including in *Life*, and nationwide on TV.

Ward also has a fire truck, together with fire helmets and red shirts for each member of the family to wear while riding it. Once, by chance, they even went to a real fire - and more people stopped to look at them than at the blaze. There'd been a birthday party for one of the Kimball youngsters, and Ward was taking his guests home on the fire truck, which also pulls an antique before-the-turn-of-the-century steam pumper. They heard the modern counterpart coming down the boulevard and turned down a side street to get out of the way. The Los Angeles County fire truck turned down the same street, and before Ward could escape, his vehicle was hemmed in by hundreds of feet of hose.

Personally, Ward is of average height and weight, with hazel eyes and a developing bald spot. He keeps physically fit by doing Yoga nearly every day, including five minutes of head standing. Also, swimming, tennis, and badminton. Sleeps about six hours a night, naps briefly at noon.

Like most of the *Interesting Railfans* in our series, he never smokes, in this case influenced by the bad example of his father having been a chain smoker. Betty doesn't smoke, either. In fact, Ward Kimball never liked to go out with a girl who smokes.

Now and then he lectures on space, art, and movie-making, and has made many TV appearances. The dozen LP albums featuring his "Firehouse 5 Plus 2 Dixie' jazz band are sold all over the world. The Kimballs are animal lovers. Their menagerie boast two Siamese cats, two finches, one lizard, three Mallard ducks, two Coral King snakes, and even a sweetwater Japanese crab.

Ward's pet peeves include phoney politics, insurance salesmen, steam-or-nothing railfans, unchained police dogs, freeway traffic, newspaper society pages, and the dearth of controversial or stimulating TV programs. Politically, he is "slightly left of center."

Says he: "I love long periods of silence: no noise, no talking, no TV, no radio. My favorite relaxation is to stretch out on a hot sandy beach and watch the crowds, seagulls, and girls go by."

His memberships include the Railway & Locomotive Historical Society, four other railfan groups, and four unions in the entertainment field. Ward likes to clown. His sense of humor is sharp, often sardonic.

Last year a 64-page book of his was published, *Art Afterpieces*, that consists of page reproductions of classic paintings by old masters in full color, each picture deftly retouched to give it a saucy or sophisticated slant. For example, Titian's *Allegory*, painted almost 500 years ago, shows a Medieval gentleman looking down over a naked woman's shoulder; Kimball slyly injected a $10 bill into his hand. The retoucher also made Whistler's Mother watch television and gave Mona Lisa a modern hair-do. Such outrages would never be forgiven by art lovers of the old school, but modern devotees find them diverting. *Art Afterpieces* may be seen on pocketbook racks all over the country.

Railfan No. 28 likes to play around with modern art, too, but not the sort that the average person fails to grasp. "I do mechanized paintings," he says, "that are built with moveable parts." One of them, Beauty Machine, is the pliable portrait of a girl which can be made attractive or not by moving her eyes and lips a fraction of an inch.

"Kimball is an uncommon man to begin with," comments the *Independent Star-News* of Pasadena, Calif., "so nothing which rolls out of his workshop surprises his friends and colleagues."

Says Ward, "I'm the kind of guy who likes to cram as much as possible into every 24 hours."

The Very First Hidden Mickey

Hidden throughout all of the Disney theme parks around the world are what are known as "Hidden Mickeys", small secretly placed references to Mickey Mouse. Hidden in the clouds, painted as part of a tree, cut into a ventilation grate, or formed into the pavement, hundreds and hundreds of these tributes to Mickey can be found in various forms, the most common of which being the "classic 3-circle" Hidden Mickey.

I had the good fortune to correspond with Disney Imagineer Terry Peterson about an element found within Disneyland, and he shared with me the story of how the very first Hidden Mickey came to be at Epcot in Walt Disney World...

"The nugget I'd most like to share is that I am the one that started the 'Hidden Mickey' gag. It has gotten blown out of proportion, but it all started with my sense of how funny it would be to find (after careful scrutiny) Mickey Mouse in the most incongruous place. I was assigned to paint a 20' high by 100' wide mural of the synapses of the brain for the "Body Wars" ride in the "Wonders of Life" attraction at Epcot. In the upper left section, there was a glob of green broccoli-looking matter and in that organic abstraction was a two square foot area that looked like Mickey's head. That was the spark that started it all. I turned it into a very realistic head of Mickey, complete with a bit of body and spaghetti-ish limbs, reaching out and blending in with the design. When I was done, as per custom, the one and only John Hench came in to look it over and

give final approval. He said "OK, great, nice work.", and I said, "I just wanna show you this first." and explained what I'd done. I said it was only paint and I just thought it would be something only the rider operators would ever see, and I could make it go away in five minutes. He said, "No, leave it. I love it!"

Hidden Mickey photo courtesy of Terry Peterson

Another Original Hidden Mickey

It's not a Disneyland story, but it's still a good one. In addition to creating the very first Hidden Mickey, Disney Imagineer Terry Peterson also created a classic and beloved Hidden Mickey that is no more. At one time, the Norway pavilion was home to the Maelstrom boat ride, which contained a small Hidden Mickey known both far and wide. As guests stood in the queue for the ride, they would've noticed a Viking ship on the left side of a large mural that depicted the history and wonders of Norway. According to Terry Peterson...

"I and three colleagues painted this 20' x 100' mural, which featured all four of us as the giant figures in the piece. While painting the Viking ship, full of men returning from their plundering, I thought it would be funny to replace one of the horned helmets with a Mickey Mouse hat that guests can purchase and wear. I inscribed it with the embroidered name "Leif", and it passed the buyoff and went on to become another fun "inside" joke." *Hidden Mickey photo courtesy of Terry Peterson*

HAND-CARVED DISNEYLAND

Found all throughout Disneyland are tributes to many different Disney notables who not only played an important role in Walt's life, but also the development of the Walt Disney Company, as well as the designing and building of Disneyland. Bob Gurr has a window with a bicycle on Main Street, U.S.A., Winsor McCay has the mutoscopes in the Penny Arcade, Giorgio Cavazzano has a plane wing in the Jungle Cruise queue, and a majestic steam engine named after Ward Kimball plys the tracks of the Disneyland Railroad. Yet one man can find tributes to his work all throughout Disneyland, and that is Disney Imagineer and master woodcarver Ray Kinman.

Many of the beautiful hand-carved wooden attraction signs, menu boards, store displays, statues, and other pieces of art that guests see in Disneyland are created by Ray. When a new piece is needed, the Imagineers contact him to discuss the scope of the project and collaborate on what they have in mind. Next, details such as design elements, colors, the materials to be used, and more are all clarified. This is then followed up with a set of blueprints sent to Ray, which convey in more specific detail what the Imagineers have in mind. As a master woodcarver, Ray has over 40 years of experience and has hand carved thousands of pieces, so the blueprint is soon put to work as he brings it to life in a new and elaborate work of Disneyland art.

Each of Ray's pieces within Disneyland has a story to tell. A favorite of his is the story behind the large Country Bear Playhouse sign, which hung in the park until September of 2001, when the attraction closed to make room for the new Many Adventures of Winnie the Pooh. The concept for the Country Bear Playhouse came about when Walt charged Imagineer Marc Davis with the task of creating a show for guests at Disney's Mineral King Ski Resort, which Walt was planning to build in California during the mid-1960s. Marc, in turn, solicited the help of fellow Imagineer Al Bertino, and together they came up with the idea of an animatronic band of bears with a southern style.

Unknown to most guests is that the lead character in this "bear band", Big Al, was based upon Al Bertino. According to his daughter, Al was so animated and gregarious that his fellow Imagineers decided to make him into the character of Big Al, and if you look closely at both the animatronic character in the band and Big Al in the sign above, you'll notice they both look exactly like Al Bertino.

It's interesting to note that the elaborate sign created for the Country Bear Playhouse almost didn't happen. Ray had been working on a canoe display for a store at Disneyland when he lost his left index finger in a chainsaw accident. The good news is that the finger was fixed, but it is almost impossible for a master woodcarver to practice his craft when his hand is healing in a cast. Of course, as life goes, this is exactly when Disney Imagineering contacted him and asked if he would carve the Country Bear Playhouse sign, an extensive project on a piece measuring nearly 7' across and over 4' high! Thankfully, a couple of friends came to his aid and helped him rough-out the piece, and Ray, using only one hand, methodically finished the sign. He clearly crafted a masterpiece, as it recently sold at auction for $85,000!

THE EARLY HISTORY OF DISNEY MERCHANDISE

Of course, it wouldn't be Disneyland without an abundance of magical merchandise for sale. Walk along Main Street, U.S.A. and you'll discover store after store and shelf after shelf filled with Mickey Mouse ears, colorful apparel, soft plush characters, toys of all kinds, jewelry, housewares, crystal arts, tasty food treats, and hundreds of other fun souvenirs all tied to Disneyland and your favorite Disney characters.

The early history leading to all of this Disneyland merchandise is a story as old as Mickey Mouse himself, and, as Walt said, it was all started by a mouse...on a children's writing tablet.

1929 - Mickey Mouse Children's Writing Tablet

In 1929, about one year after the release of Mickey's third cartoon, *Steamboat Willie*, the affable and adventurous star was beginning to take the world by storm, and while his popularity soared, Walt was focused on creating his next cartoon adventures, as well as growing the business. As a result, he hadn't given much thought to the idea of merchandising Mickey or any of his growing collection of Disney characters, but that changed in late 1929 when he was approached by a man while in a New York hotel lobby who offered him $300 for the rights to put an image of Mickey Mouse on the cover of a writing tablet for children. According to Walt in an interview years later... "*As usual, Roy and I needed money, so I took the three hundred.*" And with that, the very first Disney merchandise item was created.

Extremely Rare 1930 Mickey Mouse Children's Composition Book

1929 - Walt Disney Enterprises

Unfortunately, the name of the man who approached Walt has been lost to history, but his timing played an important role in Walt's continued success, for in August of 1929 the Great Depression struck, sending America into economic turmoil almost overnight. The stock market crashed, bank accounts simply vanished, and countless businesses large and small all across the country were forced to close. Walt was fortunate, however, for his new character, Mickey Mouse, was growing more and more famous by the day around the world, and this new opportunity created by merchandise sales would add a timely and much needed revenue stream to his business. On December 16, 1929 Walt and Roy created Walt Disney Enterprises, and through this new division they would manage the growing sales and licensing of Disney merchandise.

1930s Borgfeldt Fun-e-Flex Wooden Doll

1930 - Disney's First Licensing Agreement

Only a couple of months later, on February 3, 1930, Roy signed Walt Disney Enterprises' first licensing agreement with the Geo. Borgfeldt Corporation. Located in Manhattan, which was the center of merchandise licensing and distribution, they brought to the table 53 years of experience. Soon, they were offering retailers "the most unusual and complete line of Mickey Mouse and other Disney character merchandise", including bisque figures, wooden "Fun-e-Flex" figurines, handkerchiefs, tea sets, and more.

1932 - Walt and Roy Meet Kay Kamen

While the Geo. Borgfeldt Corporation stoked the boiler of the locomotive that would pull the train of Disney merchandise, it was a former hat salesman that would run that train down the tracks and across the globe with a full head of steam.

Herman "Kay" Kamen was a 40 year-old Merchandising Executive with an office in Kansas City, MO, the same town Walt had left only years earlier to join Roy in Los Angeles and start the Disney Brothers Cartoon Studio. He had experience developing and selling merchandise based upon the early films and animated characters of that era, and, seeing the limited reach of Disney's products at the hands of a small number of different distributors, he felt he alone could do a much better job of merchandising Walt's many characters. With this in mind, he reached out to Walt and Roy and pitched to them the idea of having him become the sole representative for Walt Disney Enterprises. They liked what they heard in Kay's pitch, so they invited him to travel out to Los Angeles to meet with them and to discuss his proposal. Kay was a bold, creative, and innovative thinker, and he knew that he had to make an even stronger pitch in Los Angeles to capture the business of the company behind one of the world's most popular stars, Mickey Mouse. Withdrawing his life's savings and sewing it into the lining of his jacket, he boarded a train for the two day trip to Los Angeles, making sure not to fall asleep along the way, lest someone steal his hidden cash.

Arriving in Los Angeles, Kay explained his idea in detail to Walt and Roy, promising not only a substantial increase in business and revenue through the use of new and innovative sales and merchandising techniques, but also a commitment to ensuring that all Disney products produced under his charge would reflect only the highest of quality. Laying his life's savings out on the table to buy the rights to the position, he told them, "*I don't know how much business you're doing, but I'll guarantee you that much business, and give you 50% of everything I do over.*" After hearing Kay's pitch, Walt and Roy excused themselves and stepped aside to have a private conversation between the two of them, where they agreed that Kay's proposal would seamlessly fit with what the two of them had in mind for the still nascent Walt Disney Enterprises. Turning around to inform Kay that he had a deal, they found him fast asleep, the result of staying awake for the past two days!

The deal that Walt, Roy, and Kay struck that day began not only a very profitable relationship which ushered in innovative new ideas, but also a warm friendship between the three of them that would continue for many years.

1934 Emerson Mickey Mouse Model 411 Radio

1933 - Kay Kamen Incorporated

Kay was a man who knew where he wanted to go and how to get there. Come the following year, he had opened Kay Kamen, Incorporated in New York so as to be in the heart of the action near the offices of major merchandise manufacturers and importers. Here, he, along with his staff of 20 sales representatives and in-house artists, negotiated the deals, built the relationships, and provided the sales materials that would double Disney's merchandise sales to over $6 million within only 6 months. Soon, department stores, toy stores, five and dimes, boutiques, bookstores, and countless other retailers across the globe were generating profits amidst the grip of the great depression from the sale of hundreds of different kinds of Disney merchandise items, including figurines, toys, stuffed dolls, jewelry, furniture, apparel, school supplies, radios, record players, greeting cards, books, tablets, and more.

1934 Kay Kamen Catalog - First Edition

1934 - Mickey Mouse Merchandise Catalogs

Kay Kamen was not only driven, he was also an innovator, and one of his early innovations was the introduction of his first Mickey Mouse Merchandise catalog in 1934, the "first of its kind in the history of merchandising." Filled with 76 pages of products produced by 49 different licensees, it offered a wealth of Mickey Mouse branded items, including savings banks, sheepskin moccasins, toothbrushes, pop-up books, bisque figurines, tricycles, play tents and pillows, canvas shoes and much more, all promoted with compelling black and white photographic detail.

This first catalog proved to be extremely successful, and it was a driving force in placing Mickey Mouse and other Disney related character merchandise in hundreds of retail stores throughout America and the world, thus driving a total of $35 million in sales by 1935. Because of its success, Kay Kamen published additional catalogs on a near yearly basis until 1949, when, sadly, he and his wife were killed in a plane crash on the Azores archipelago in the mid-Atlantic.

1930 Mickey Mouse Composition Book, 1934 Kay Kamen Mickey Mouse Merchandise Catalog, 1934 Emerson Mickey Mouse Model 411 radio, and Borgfeldt Fun-E-Flex Mickey Mouse figure: Author's collection.

THE $300 "MYSTERY MAN"

Children's Writing Tablet
The Very First Disney Merchandise Item
Tablet Photo © Edward Bergen Collection

In the world of Disney merchandise, there exists a great mystery, one which to this day, even after considerable research, nobody has been able to solve... "Who was the man who approached Walt in a New York hotel lobby in 1929 and offered him $300 for the rights to put Mickey Mouse on the cover of a children's writing tablet?"

At one point, it was believed that the mystery man was an employee of either the Powers Paper Co., which manufactured paper tablets and composition books for use by school children, or the American Lithographic Company, which, as you can imagine, created lithographic artwork. In looking into this mystery, I reached out to the Disney Consumer Products Archives division, who informed me that recent research into Disney's earliest merchandise projects casts doubts on the likelihood of the man being employed by either company.

Now, Disney knows their stuff, but my supposition, *with only very little circumstantial evidence to support it,* is that Occam's Razor applies here, and that the $300 mystery man did, indeed, work for the Powers Paper Company. Consider the following points:

- In 1929, Manhattan was considered to be *the* center of global merchandise distribution and licensing, with the International Toy Center, a complex of buildings located in the Flatiron District, being a hub for offices run by toy manufacturers and distributors.

- The Powers Paper Co., which was founded in 1857 and had been manufacturing paper products for 72 years by that point, had its headquarters in Springfield, MA, but also had an office located at 200 Fifth Avenue in New York, which is the address for the International Toy Center complex. It would have been relatively easy and convenient for a representative of the Powers Paper Co., upon hearing Walt was in town, to make his way over to Walt's hotel and pitch the idea for the children's tablet.

- Walt and Roy created a new division of their company, Walt Disney Enterprises, on December 16, 1929 to manage and license Disney merchandise.

- The first Disney merchandise product, the children's writing tablet, was first produced in 1930, as evidenced by the "© 1930 - Walter E. Disney" imprint on it's cover.

- The initial license to manufacture the Mickey Mouse children's tablet was the informal $300 handshake deal. The Powers Paper Co. obtained an *official* license to manufacture Mickey Mouse related tablets and composition books of different designs beginning in 1931, and this ran until 1940. The Powers Paper Co. *may* have begun manufacturing the initial tablets in 1930 under the $300 handshake deal while negotiating the more formal agreement, which began in 1931.

- All of the tablets manufactured by the Powers Paper Co. had an artistic style which differed noticeably from the first children's tablets produced...*except for one tablet*, and this could be a very important clue to the mystery!

- In Kay Kamen's 1934 Mickey Mouse Merchandise catalog, the Powers Paper Co. has a two page spread showcasing a collection of its different writing tablets and composition books for school children. All of the tablets and books displayed have a similar design, *except for one*, which appears in the upper left hand corner of the two page spread. This one tablet's design and artistic style differs noticeably from the rest of the Powers Paper Co. tablets and instead *matches more closely the artistic style of the first and initial tablets produced under the $300 handshake deal.* Of note are the similarities of the graphic elements of the globe, as well as a geometric shape, in this case a large rectangle drawn in the image background, which is an artistic component that was used with the initial tablet designs, but not with any of the later Powers Paper Co. designs.

Of course, if we could see the lower left hand corner of the tablet appearing in the Kay Kamen catalog, we might find the same "© 1930 - Walter E. Disney" imprint we find on the initial tablets, and this would possibly solve this riddle, but as fate would have it, this nearly 90 year-old image holds fast to the mystery!

MICKEY & MINNIE MOUSE SAVE THE DAY!

As you enter Disneyland, one of the very first things you'll see as you look up at the Disneyland Railroad Main Street Station is the Kalamazoo Hand Car sitting on the passing track, a brightly colored piece of Walt's railroad story that has welcomed guests to the park since 1956.

This isn't the only hand car in the Walt Disney railroad story, however, for another hand car owned by Walt's pal Mickey saved the day for a beloved American company that faced hard times and nearly went out of business during the Great Depression.

In 1900, a young Joshua Lionel Cowen founded the Lionel Manufacturing Company with the goal of manufacturing miniature trains for use as a means to attract attention to retailers' storefront windows. However, store owners quickly found that customers weren't coming into their stores to buy what was on display in their windows, but instead they wanted to place an order for the miniature Lionel trains! Before he knew it, Mr. Cowen was selling toy trains and their detailed accessories to parents of children all across America, and by the late 1920s, The Lionel Company had become the leading manufacturer of toy trains in America, as well as overseas.

Unfortunately, the Great Depression of 1929 brought sales to a halt, as few families had the money available to buy such luxury items as toy trains. New locomotives, rolling stock, and layout pieces were produced in an attempt to drive sales, and even non-train items, such as a toy stove, were introduced so as to cater to girls and their mothers, but times were too difficult, and by May of 1934 The Lionel Company had gone into receivership and was facing bankruptcy.

While Lionel was struggling, two years earlier, in 1932, sales and marketing genius Herman "Kay" Kamen approached Walt and Roy Disney and boldly proposed that he begin handling all of the merchandising for Disney's animated characters worldwide, including Mickey Mouse. Appreciating his drive, as well as his plan to improve the standard of quality for all of Disney's merchandise, Walt and Roy accepted Kay's terms and soon all three were involved in not only a valued friendship, but also a very profitable business deal, as Kay created countless new merchandising opportunities for Walt's characters, generating millions of dollars in revenue.

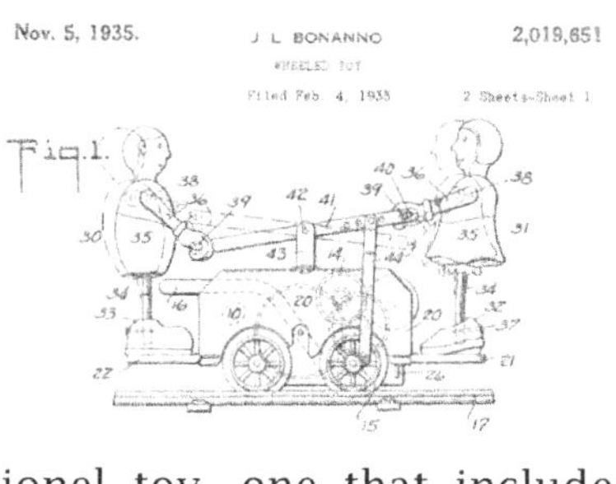

In 1934, Kay saw an opportunity for Disney and Lionel to join forces and produce a product together, and the Mickey and Minnie Mouse Hand Car was born. Priced at only $1.00, families could again afford to buy a Lionel toy, one that included a wind-up hand car in red or green, a circular O-gauge track, and two of the most famous characters in the world at the controls, Mickey and Minnie Mouse. The toy was an instant and wildly popular hit, selling one million units in about a year's time, thus saving The Lionel Company from bankruptcy and allowing it to continue down the tracks to create treasured memories for millions of families across America and around the world.

MICKEY & MINNIE MOUSE SAVE THE DAY...AGAIN!

Like The Lionel Company, the good fortunes of the world-famous Ingersoll-Waterbury Watch Company had come to a halt because of the great depression, to the point where it also had been forced to enter bankruptcy protection as a means to save the company's few remaining assets.

As he had with the Mickey & Minnie Lionel Handcar, Kay Kamen spotted another potentially very lucrative opportunity and, in 1933, he approached the beleaguered Ingersoll-Waterbury company with the idea of creating a wristwatch and pocket watch, both featuring Mickey Mouse on their faces with his yellow-gloved hands pointing to the time. Again, Kay's intuition proved to be right, as the watches were an instant hit, with Macy's selling 11,000 units in only one day! Bolstered by Mickey's growing worldwide fame, the time pieces continued to be popular, selling over 2½ million units over the next two years. In turn, the ensuing revenue allowed The Ingersoll-Waterbury Watch Company to avoid bankruptcy and instead expand its payroll during the heart of the depression from 200 employees to over 3,000 in the span of only a few weeks.

THE 10 MILLIONTH GUEST OF THE DISNEYLAND RAILROAD

Left to Right - R.G. Rydin, EVP of the Santa Fe Railway, Raymond Sleeper, and Walt Disney

Above is a press photo of Walt Disney, R.G. Rydin, and 8 year-old Raymond Sleeper, who, as luck would have it, found himself amid considerable fanfare as he became the 10 millionth guest to ride aboard the Santa Fe Disneyland Railroad, a milestone rewarded by Walt when he presented young Raymond with a special commemorative boxcar filled with 10,000 pennies. As I recently read about this story, I wondered whatever happened to Raymond, the boxcar, and all of those pennies, but my initial research uncovered very little about him or his big day at Disneyland. As a result, I set out to find Raymond...over 60 years later...to answer these questions. It took some searching, but I found him, and what follows is his story, told for the first time in any Disney-related books, articles, or web sites...

In mid-summer of 1960, Mr. & Mrs. Sleeper were in the process of moving their young family from Hawaii to Maryland, as Mr. Sleeper, who was a Colonel in the U.S. Air Force, was being transferred to Andrews Air Force Base. Reaching California, the plan was to drive across country in their new baby blue Rambler station wagon, but first a trip to Disneyland was in order. On the morning of August 3rd, the Rambler pulled into the busy Disneyland parking lot, and inside, 8 year-old Raymond, his sister, and his four brothers grew antsy with excitement and anticipation as Disneyland's Main Street Station came into view. This was their very first trip to the park. Little did they know, they were about to experience a special moment of Disney magic, which they would all remember for the rest of their lives.

Piling from the car, Raymond and his siblings all gazed upon the majestic train station gleaming in the California sunshine high above the entrance gates. Guests gathered in line at the turnstiles to get into the park, and somewhere in the distance a train whistle announced the impending arrival of the Ernest S. Marsh locomotive, finishing yet another journey from such distant places as Adventureland, Frontierland, Tomorrowland, and beyond. Raymond remembers what happened next...

"I recall my father saying, 'We should ride the railroad around the park first, to get an idea of what we can see and what we want to do for the day.'

Once inside, my two younger brothers and I raced for the Santa Fe & Disneyland Railroad Station. I was 8 and arrived first at the turnstile for the next train, followed by my younger brother, Harry, who was 6, and my youngest brother, Grant, who was 5. When the rest of the group arrived, I let Grant get in front of me so that he could be first in line. Seeing this, Harry began grumbling about his being younger than me, so I let him in front of me, too. It was then that I noticed that the ticket takers and others seemed to be paying close attention to us as we waited in line, talking to each other as they kept an eye us. When we were let through the turnstile, some cast members pulled us all aside and began excitedly speaking to my parents, letting them know that something special had just happened...I was the 10 millionth guest on the Santa Fe & Disneyland Railroad, and I was about to be awarded a magical prize, a unique box car filled with 10,000 pennies, along with a Revell HO model railroad set!

Raymond Sleeper receives a special HO scale model train and layout from Walt Disney
Photo: Don Erb - Santa Fe Railway

Shortly after they spoke with my parents, they approached me and told me that I was a special guest for the day, one who had just won 10,000 pennies, which was a lot of money for an 8 year-old boy. In addition, I was named Honorary Vice-President of the Santa Fe Disneyland Railroad. Needless to say, my siblings were less than pleased, especially Grant and Harry, who I had let go before me in line. Soon, Walt had joined us, along with Engineer Bill, while the Disneyland Band added some lively Disney music to help mark this special occasion.

There were about half a dozen photographers there, and they had us pose for some photos, both in the cab of the Ernest S. Marsh and with the boxcar filled with bright and shiny pennies. After that, I got to ride in the cab and 'drive' the train around the park, which was a highlight of the entire ceremony. We went around Disneyland only once, stopping at all the stops.

Raymond, Walt, & Engineer Bill,
a local TV personality, pose aboard the Ernest S. Marsh

Afterwards, a young woman took us on a tour of the park. We rode all the rides we wanted to ride, and I don't remember having to wait in any lines. Later in the day, while riding in the wheelhouse of the Mark Twain Riverboat, mom suggested that I let Harry pilot the boat, since he had been whining that he should have been the winner that day.

After Raymond's big day, his family continued on to Maryland. The boxcar and pennies would arrive soon afterward, having been shipped from Disneyland.

Disneyland fans will want to know... "So, whatever happened to the boxcar and 10,000 pennies?" Raymond opened his very first bank account with all of the pennies once he arrived in Maryland, and the boxcar was ultimately stored in the garage of the family home, along with the Revell HO scale Santa Fe Electric Train Set he had also received from Walt that day. Unfortunately, a house fire in the fall of 1970 consumed both the boxcar and the train set, leaving nothing of either, only memories of a very special day for a lucky 8 year-old boy at Disneyland.

Raymond opens his first bank account with his 10,000 pennies, accompanied by his unique Disneyland boxcar

THE FIRST DISNEYLAND LOCOMOTIVE

By Disney Legend Bob Gurr

Walt was a master at storytelling, be it in the high-flying adventures of Mickey Mouse in *Plane Crazy*, the grand sweeping score of Fantasia, or even the authentic sights and sounds of the Disneyland Railroad.

In July of 1954, construction began on Walt's new Disneyland, and since Walt wanted the park surrounded by a train, work also began on two locomotives which were to be designed and built from the ground up in time to ply the rails on Disneyland's opening day, less than one year away. Here is a story, graciously shared by Disney Legend Bob Gurr, which describes some of the work which occurred behind the scenes to place the very first Disneyland locomotive on the tracks.

When Roger Broggie set me to work on the Autopia, he gave me a drafting board in a room with some interesting "olde tyme" characters from America's railroad past...steam freaks, I called them. We seemed worlds apart; they were mostly in their 50s to 70s, while I was a green kid of 22. Steam railroads where their passion, sports cars and airplanes were my big thrill. The whole bunch had a leader, Earl Vilmer, a railroad superintendent with over 20 years experience. Real quiet guy, hired by Roger Broggie to head up the whole Disneyland Railroad effort. Another quiet but very funny guy, a model railroader named Eddie Sargeant, was drafting up all the railroad cars. Everyone's favorite animator-steam guru-band leader Ward Kimball was always there to kibbutz. Another combination model railroad guy and story writer was Dick Bagley. Roger had him drafting up the steam engines for the Mark Twain sternwheeler riverboat. But the fellow who took me under his wing and mentored me into the "world of steam" was the pixie-like Ed Lingenfelter. Ed was born back in the 19th century and loved the great monster steam engines as a kid. He learned his engineering trade very early and spent an entire career designing steam locomotives in Pennsylvania. Years after retirement, Ed was hired by Walt to engineer the 5/8 scale Lilly Belle Locomotive.

To get the hang of proper drafting format, Ed had a big chart on his wall explaining the essence of good design communication. He showed me how many ways there were to explain something to a machinist with a blueprint. All the other guys were cranking out tons of locomotive and railroad car drawings. Eddie Sargeant did most of the rolling stock. Earl Vilmer would stop and draw anything needed as well as act as the lead superintendent. Old records show that Earl made drawings starting on December 31, 1954, Sargeant got started on August 14, 1954. Ed started the locomotive erecting diagram on July 30, 1954, but Bagley got going on July 2, 1954. Ed even gave me the headlight reflector to draw up for the Lilly Belle on May 27, 1955.

Ed was amazing; he would draw all the locomotive parts first, get them to the shop, then calculate the design afterwards. Seemed backwards, but he just knew everything about steam by heart. And steam is real tricky when you change scale from full size down to Walt's own Lilly Belle, then back up to 5/8 size. And what a storyteller!

Soon, the first Disneyland locomotive was ready to steam up in the round house. Walt opened the throttle a bit but nothing moved. A bit more and the new locomotive almost silently glided forward. *"No, no, no! Go fix it."*...Walt exclaimed. I was puzzled, so I asked Ed to explain. He chuckled and told me that locomotives have machining clearances expressed as "either tight or loose 1/64ths of an inch." It seems the Studio Machine Shop did a fine job and revised some tolerances to thousandths of an inch. After all, the shop did build precise movie cameras. Ed had warned that his dimensions should apply, so he got a big laugh out of the effort to disassemble the tight parts and open them up. A few days later the locomotive clunked and clanked out of the barn just like a proper locomotive should, using just a tiny bit of throttle. *"Yes."*...said Walt. Naturally, Earl Vilmer and all the steam freaks in attendance smiled and nodded in their conservative silence. To this day, I cherish the knowledge I learned from those wonderful wizards whose world was so far from mine.

ACKNOWLEDGMENTS

Many people have graciously contributed to the development of this book. From Marty Sklar's information about the early days of *The Disneyland News* to Bob Gurr's stories and generous comments, as well as Michael Broggie's and Michael Campbell's help with details, photos and a couple of great new stories, many have played a role, large or small, in helping me write a title that contains not only quality content, but also family value entertainment which is respectful of the legacy of Walt Disney and Disneyland.

For that, I would like to thank you all...

- Bob Gurr - Disney Legend and Imagineer
- Brian Hillman - George H. Lloyd Relative
- Brian & Meghan Westby - Research Technicians
- Cindy Bothner - Walt Disney Imagineering
- Dave Drumheller - WDWGuidedTours.com
- David Lesjak - Disney Historian and Author
- Frank Reifsnyder - Walt Disney Imagineering
- George Eldridge - Decoding the Disneyland Telegraph
- Glenn Barker - Walt Disney Imagineering
- Jeff Kober - PerformanceJourneys.com
- Jordan Sallis - George H. Lloyd Relative
- Kristy Westby - Research Technician
- Marty Sklar - Principal Creative Executive for The Walt Disney Company
- Megan Westby - Disneyland Photographer
- Michael & Sharon Broggie - Disney Historians and Authors
- Michael Campbell - President Emeritus, Carolwood Pacific Historical Society
- Mike Westby - Disney App and Guidebook Author
- Ray Kinman - Disney Imagineer
- Steve DeGaetano - Disneyland Railroad Historian - SteamPassages.com
- Terry Peterson - Disney Imagineer
- The Disney Archives

And most of all my parents, Richard & Roberta, for taking me to Disneyland for the very first time many years ago!

THE HIDDEN SECRETS & STORIES OF DISNEYLAND

"Almost every page contained details I had never noticed before."

- Disney Legend Bob Gurr

If you enjoyed reading these in-depth details about Disneyland, then you're sure to enjoy *The Hidden Secrets & Stories of Disneyland*. The companion book to this title, it is a fun and entertaining look at **over 250** of the magical secrets and story elements hidden by the Disney Imagineers throughout Disneyland...all arranged as a fun tour and complete with **more than 220** photos!

Available online. Learn more at:

www.Disney-Secrets.com

The Hidden Secrets & Stories of Walt Disney World

The Hidden Secrets & Stories of Walt Disney World is an entertaining and magical in-depth look at the secret details and story elements the Disney Imagineers have purposely hidden throughout Walt Disney World for guests to find and enjoy...all arranged as a fun tour and complete with photos!

Through countless park visits, interviews, and untold hours of in-depth research, *The Hidden Secrets & Stories of Walt Disney World* presents over **500** fun, whimsical, and fascinating details, including never-before-published stories and photos.

Available online. Learn more at:

www.Disney-Secrets.com

Walt Disney's Railroad Story

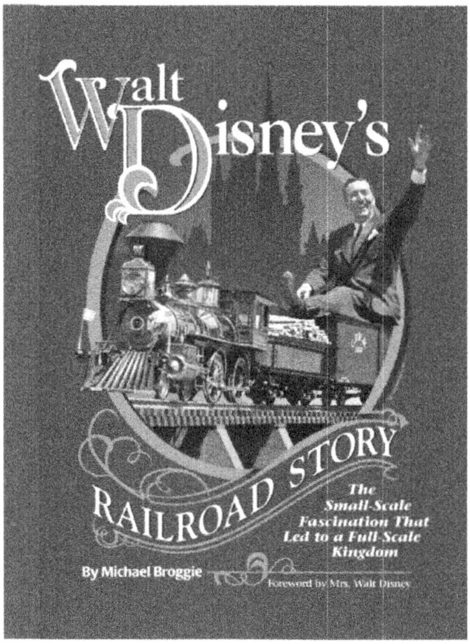

Michael Broggie's masterpiece, *Walt Disney's Railroad Story*, captures in fascinating detail every facet of Walt's life-long passion with steam trains, from his days marveling at powerful steam locomotives as a child in Marceline, MO and his work as News Butcher as a 14 year-old boy on the Missouri Pacific line, to his own miniature backyard railroad, the Carolwood Pacific, and the beautiful trains which encircle every Disney theme park around the world today. Featuring never-before-published photos and interviews with Mrs. Walt Disney, Diane Disney Miller, Ward Kimball, Ollie Johnston, Bob Harpur, Bill Cottrell, Roger Broggie, Bill Evans and many others. Hardcover Edition - Color - 432 Pages - 350 Pictures

Available online. Learn more by visiting:

www.Carolwood.com

WALT DISNEY'S FIRST SUPERSTAR: MICKEY MOUSE

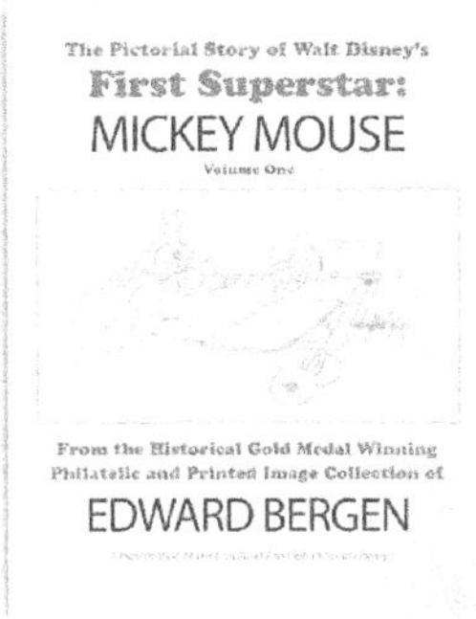

From the historical Gold Medal winning philatelic and printed image collection of Edward Bergen comes three captivating books which chronicle the early days of Mickey Mouse's rise as a global phenomenon and beloved cultural icon. Browse through large full colored images of some of the finest examples available of extremely rare Mickey Mouse artifacts from 1928 through the 1940s, including original animation artwork, postcards, letters, greeting cards, books, magazines, novelties, toys, wristwatches, and much more. You'll discover beautiful domestic and international pieces, as well as an example of the very first Mickey Mouse merchandise product ever produced.

To learn more, and to order your own signed copies,
send an email to Edward Bergen at:

revcorvette1@yahoo.com

SELECTED BIBLIOGRAPHY

Many sources of content, including interviews, books, articles, documents, vintage publications, photos, correspondence, video and of course countless theme park visits were used in the research for this book.

Here are some publications which were not only helpful, but I would highly recommend them as reading material for anyone interested in Disneyland, Walt Disney World or Disney history...

Broggie, Michael. *Walt Disney's Railroad Story.* Donning Company Publishers, 4th Edition. 2014

DeGaetano, Steve. *The Disneyland Railroad - A Complete History in Words and Pictures.* Collector's Edition

Gabler, Neal. *Walt Disney: The Triumph of the American Imagination.* Alfred A. Knopf, 2006

Lloyd, George. *George H. Lloyd's Hand Carved Caenstone Model of Our National Capitol.* Lowenstein's, Approx. 1943

Sklar, Marty. *Dream It! Do It!: My Half-Century Creating Disney's Magic Kingdoms.* Disney Editions, 2013

Smith, Dave. *Disney A to Z: The Updated Official Encyclopedia.* Disney Editions, 1998

Lesjak, David. *In The Service Of The Red Cross - Walt Disney's Early Adventures - 1918 - 1919*

Thomas, Bob. *Walt Disney: An American Original.* Hyperion, 1994

www.MechanicalMusicPress.com